My Many Sisters

My Many Sisters

The Journal of a Volunteer with the Daughters of Charity

Caroline Watanabe

The people mentioned in this book are real, though many of the names have been changed.

ISBN: 978-0-9827514-9-7
Library of Congress Control Number: 2011930390

Cover Photographs: Caroline Watanabe
Interior Photographs: Caroline Watanabe and her Friends in Taiwan
Manufactured in the United States of America

Ink Brush Press
Temple and Dallas, Texas

For the Daughters of Charity
and
all those who give their lives in the service of others

Nonfiction from Ink Brush Press

Jim McGarrah, *The End of an Era.* This is an insightful, heartbreaking and, at times, hilarious account of Jim McGarrah's struggles as a veteran in the aftermath of the Vietnam War.

Robert Rynearson, *Time to Listen.* Dr. Robert Rynearson describes Profile Self Confrontation, a counseling technique in which patients view on video screen the right and left profiles of their own faces. *Time to Listen* also chronicles Dr. Rynearson's personal journey into studying medicine and psychiatry and, ultimately, into his work with Profile Self Confrontation.

William Seale, *Texas Riverman.* In this remarkable biography, Dr. Seale gives a lively account of Captain Andrew Smyth, whose life spanned the history of Texas river transportation from the 1830s to the 1870s, from rafts to flatboats to keelboats and finally to steamboats.

Charles Taylor, *Saving Sebastian.* Dr. Charles Taylor's latest book is a moving but gritty memoir of his struggles with his son's drug and alcohol addiction.

For more information on these and Ink Brush Press books of fiction and poetry, go to www.inkbrushpress.com

Introduction

I was born in Osaka, Japan. My mother is Caucasian American and my father is Japanese. Until I started the first grade my parents made it a rule that my mother would speak to me only in English, while my father would speak to me only in Japanese. It worked out well, and I was bilingual by the time I could talk.

After going to the first grade in a Japanese school, my English started to slip. It was then that my parents decided that in our home we will speak only English. My upbringing included occasional visits to the United States. The result was that I became bilingual, bicultural, and binational. When I started high school, I quit the Japanese school and began to homeschool in English because I wanted to go to a university in America, and Japanese schools, while good at teaching English, could not help me with English as much as could homeschooling.

My homeschool program required a foreign language, and at first I chose Spanish, but I could not understand the concepts without a teacher there with me, for the grammar was entirely new. I looked into different languages, and decided Mandarin Chinese was a good choice because that language shares grammatical elements of both Japanese and English. The Chinese characters were familar; perhaps 30% of them are the same as Japanese kanji characters I learned as a child.

So I came up with the idea of going to China to continue learning Mandarin.

So I came up with the idea of going to China to continue learning Mandarin. I had been studying Chinese for about a year at this point. My mother suggested making contact with a religious community and mission where I might serve as a volunteer; doing so would improve my language skills, and and I could be helpful to other people in some way.

I talked to the sister at the church my family attends. The sister was a member of the Daughters of Charity. When I asked about the possibility of my going to Taiwan or China, she put me in touch with the superior of the Taiwanese community for the Daughters of Charity.

Going to mainland China was out of the question since there was not such a Christian community in China that felt safe for me to visit because of strict laws governing Christian groups. The idea of going to Taiwan became increasingly attractive as I found out more about the Daughters of Charity in Taiwan, their missionary work, and languages. The languages they spoke in that community were mainly English and Mandarin. Also, because the Japanese military had occupied Taiwan for half a century—until 1945—many older people in Taiwan spoke Japanese. So a full year before going to Taiwan, I had the trip planned. My Taiwanese adventures began in January, 2010.

As I write this it has been almost a year since my experience in Taiwan, and my knowledge of Mandarin Chinese is fading a bit. After spending 6 months in the United States for university study —my first time in the U.S. for such a long period—English now dominates my linguistic life, and studying Mandarin has been replaced with learning Italian at the University of Dallas.

Though my primary goal in going to Taiwan was to get comfortable with Chinese, what I gained from going was more than any language could offer. What happened to me in Taiwan now feels something like what happens to a baby when it starts to walk. The process does not come from force of conscious will or systematic training. For a baby, being able to walk gives an entirely new perspective on the world since the height, sight, and most of all the ability to reach things once unreachable opens up possibilities unimaginable before. But of course I cannot remember how it felt to walk for the first time, and now it is impossible to articulate completely the emotional impact of my experience in Taiwan.

When people asked me why I was going to Taiwan, I said that I was going to solidify my Chinese while helping others in some small way. But another motive for going, one I didn't see clearly myself, was a desire to force myself out of my comfort zone, to test myself on how strong I really was, and to learn how being bicultural might affect my perceptions of cultures I am unfamiliar with. I gave little thought about hardships that I might experience in Taiwan, nor did I have high expectations. In fact, I had no expectations at all, which was useful, for I was not disappointed with anything. Now, in retrospect, one goal was to gain wider experience with living, which is something I did, and this journal is a testimony to that.

大成坊

1/19

I woke up a couple of times during the first night in my new bed. I kept trying to change my position to be more comfortable, but it's hard to do on a hospital bed.

I'm staying at a convent with the Daughters of Charity in Tainan, a town in southern Taiwan. It's not a beautiful place. The buildings are all crammed together and the air is polluted. You see the bikers with their anti-pollution air masks on all the time. You can walk in a straight line down the street and buy everything you need without turning the corner. There seems to be no crime, so even a young girl like me can walk at night and feel safe. I'm told the people here are nicer than those in northern Taiwan. When they meet my eye, they tilt their heads in respect or smile, seeing as I am a foreigner in their city.

My alarm went off at 6:45 a.m. and Mass is at 7:00. Today is my first day as a volunteer, and this morning I didn't know what I'd be doing. This is a home for the elderly, and there are many specialists working here to do their particular chores. I hope they will spare me an easy job or two so I won't feel totally useless. I set my alarm so that I'd have just enough time to brush my teeth and hair and put on some clean clothes, but I noticed after going to the chapel that getting to work exactly on time is a mistake. There are many elderly people in wheelchairs needing help and waiting in the chapel. I felt guilty knowing I could have gotten up earlier to help. And the other workers—were they already labeling me as too young, too selfish, and useless?

And the other workers—were they already labeling me as too young, too selfish, and useless?

I sat next to an American sister, Sr. Annie. She is a jolly woman, already over seventy years old, but active and strong. Two Chinese men wearing priest's clothing sat in wheelchairs. At first I thought they would be saying Mass, and I wondered how a person in a wheelchair would reach the top of the altar. Then another priest walked in, white-haired, but standing. Three priests saying Mass at 7:00 in the morning on Tuesday, I thought. This is going to be an unusual experience.

They said the Mass in Chinese, of course. I had my own manual in English. I tried to follow the sounds, but I didn't understand much because I'm lost without the Chinese characters to read. Thus, my mind often wandered, and I felt guilty for doing that during prayer.

The priest in front to my left sat in a wheelchair. As we all stood up to pray and follow the lead of the priest, I saw that he clenched his hands and had his feet in an odd position in the wheelchair. Was he wishing he could stand beside his friend? Maybe wishing he could say Mass again without the disabilities that came to him in old age? At that moment I wondered how much these priests and sisters have sacrificed in order to be religious. But then again, I thought, maybe it's we, the lay people, who avoid being more religious by choosing not to make such sacrifices.

During Mass, Sr. Annie tugged at my sleeve and pointed out an old woman sitting in the front. She wore a brownish knit hat and held a rosary. I had noticed her when I came in because I thought she was saying the rosary. Her toothless mouth kept mumbling words I could not hear.

"She's a hundred years old," Sr. Annie whispered to me.

One hundred years old, I marveled, and she gets up early in the morning to pray, to say her rosary while I, so young, supposedly full of energy, do not get up early. I wondered how much she could understand now, at such a great age. Her mumbling and fumbling with her rosary and her strange looking face without teeth made her unique among the old people I saw this morning. Was her show of faith mere habit, muscle memory maybe, or was she fully present in her show of loyalty to the church? And yet there seemed to be something in her eyes that caused me to think she managed to maintain true faith in this, her hundredth year. The thought gave me comfort and hope.

The ceremony confounded me with a language I had studied but could not yet follow, so I read the passages in my English manual. In the middle of the service it became clear that I had read the wrong ones, so I flipped pages until I found the right ones. I hoped Sr. Annie didn't notice.

As the Mass ended, I tried to help everyone go back to their rooms. I helped the man sitting behind me stand up and get his cane. He smiled at me. I smiled back. Though I may not yet understand their language, the universal language of a smile can always work.

It was breakfast time, and I was quite hungry. I ate two pieces of a sweet bread that tasted like cheese. I had fruit, too; there was plenty of that.

The sisters here are funny when they speak English, especially Sr. Elaine. When she laughs, everyone laughs with her, in part because she sort of resembles a koi fish with glasses, a sight that makes her laughter even funnier. Her gesticulations and her accented English can make anyone laugh in a good way.

Last night, Sr. Stella told me a story of a Japanese sister who went to mainland China and died because she ate something she shouldn't have. After that the Japanese refused to send anyone to China for a long time. She asked me please to be careful, that if I accidently ate something lethal—a peanut, maybe—and died in Taiwan, Japanese families would never again send their girls as volunteers to work in Taiwan. She seemed so serious in her lecture, then she cracked a mischievous smile and crinkled her eyes, and we all had a good laugh. Later in bed I thought how strange it is that a dreary subject like death could end up being cheerful just because of the way Sr. Stella told her story.

The sisters like to talk about old age and subjects related to age. They tease each other about how each is becoming more forgetful. With their good humor and good facial expressions, they manage to make me laugh, and they poke fun at each other about who is older and more forgetful.

The sisters like to talk about old age and subjects related to age. They tease each other about how each is becoming more forgetful.

Sr. Stella introduced me to the staff of the home. She told them that I was half Japanese and half American. Their first word to me

The top floor and part of the roof served for the laundry room and clotheslines.

was *piaoliang*, which means "pretty." I smiled at them and said thank you. Their response was surprising because I had taken no time to put on makeup that morning, so they were looking at the true me, and yet they said *piaoliang* with sincerity. Maybe they thought that because I have a different face, an Amerasian face, one they're not used to and don't know how to judge, or maybe they spoke the word just to have something to say, and maybe I don't want to know their reasons.

There are five floors to the building. The fifth floor is the place where they fold and wash laundry, especially the diapers for the older people. The view from the windows was as nice as a polluted city can get. I could see only about one or two kilometers, then everything became hazy. The fourth floor is for the people who need most help, such as having to have feeding tubes. Some are completely bedridden. There is more activity on the third floor, but many there suffer from dementia. The people on the second floor are more alert, and I got to speak Japanese with some of them. They all welcomed me, shook my hand, and told me I was pretty again and again. I wanted to tell them they were pretty, too, with their toothless yet charming smiles, but thought better of it. It was true about their smiles. The smile of a really elderly person is as nice as you can see on a person of any age.

Being introduced to the elderly people was the most rewarding time of the day. Their smiles of welcome and their effort to speak Japanese to me got me to smile from the heart. That was the first of many times that I wished I could speak better Chinese.

When the tour finished, Sr. Stella asked what job I would like. She admitted there wasn't much I could do since there is a language barrier. I told her I would do anything, and I agreed to go to the fifth floor and help fold laundry. I liked it up there, and I didn't want to cause any stress and trouble for the workers downstairs, who were mainly women who spoke no English or Japanese.

So there I was in the morning, folding diapers. They were all clean, of course, and it felt satisfying to see the piles of unfolded ones getting smaller and smaller. The man who worked with the laundry could speak good English, so I had a few conversations with him. He is Taiwanese, but lived in Canada about fifteen years ago. He also managed to remind me, perhaps without intending to, that I am quite young. Maybe I could think of myself as old among some of my friends in Japan or America, but in that building there was no way I could think of myself as old. Perspective certainly can shift.

Around 11:30 I went walking around again since my laundry was done for the time being. I tried finding Sr. Paula, a Filipina woman. She's quite old, but still bright and sharp. She can speak good English, and I like her company. I couldn't find her in the elderly folks' home, so I returned to the sisters' home where the cook was making lunch.

As is the custom among many Filipinos, Sr. Paula pointed with her lips instead of using fingers.

I tried conversing with the cook while I had lunch, but that didn't go so well. All I could think to talk about was how good the food was and to ask about her family. The conversation felt limited, small, and lacking because of my limited ability to speak her language. We kept misunderstanding each other, and I felt bad because I could tell she wanted to help me understand.

Lunch break seemed to go on and on. When I realized how much time everyone took off for lunch, I went to the fifth floor with my books to study a bit. I found out afterwards that many people take a nap during lunch time, and lunch break does not end until 2:00 p.m.

At two o'clock I folded more diapers with Sr. Paula, who often works on the fifth floor. I found out she had fifteen brothers and sisters and that two of them died while she was in Taiwan. She's been here for the past fifty years or so. Her father married another woman after Sr. Paula's "first mother" died as a young woman.

As is the custom among many Filipinos, Sr. Paula pointed with her lips instead of using fingers. I smiled, remembering my visit to the Philippines when my friend Sonny told me that people point with their mouths there.

Such memories made me miss my friends and family back home. What would they think of me now? They would probably laugh and make fun of me for folding people's diapers. It amused me to think what my fiancé would say—if I had a fiancé—if I said, "I've never been married, but I'm a pro at folding diapers."

Sr. Paula invited me to a three o'clock rosary, and I helped set up a microphone so the elderly could hear. About ten to fifteen people in wheelchairs gathered around Sr. Paula as she began to say the rosary. I followed her Chinese some and began making sense of some of her words. I sat in front, beside an old woman who could still walk. Sr. Paula told me the woman is a Franciscan nun.

When I moved my chair closer to the front, the Franciscan nun grabbed my shirttail and pulled it down. Maybe she thought part of my pants pockets and most of my bottom shouldn't be seen. I thanked her, sat down, and tried talking to her; but she couldn't hear what I was saying so I gave up.

The rosary lasted about twenty minutes, and I was embarrassed to realize that my mind wandered. I had been thinking about the earthquake in Haiti and about those who died, and the idea of writing my thoughts down as a journal came to me at that moment. If some heavenly being put that thought into my head, that "being" better have some good reason for motivating me because I'm going to be sleep deprived tomorrow from writing all this down!

With rosary time over, I went with Sr. Paula back to the nuns' house and ate some oranges. I offered her some, but she said it was too sweet for her, as she cut into a piece of sugary bread. She ate about a fourth of the bread before admitting it was quite sweet, probably sweeter than the orange I had offered her. Funny old people, I thought, then felt oddly guilty for the thought.

When I went back outside with Sr. Paula, we found many of the residents doing some exercise or sitting in the sun. Staff members helped many of them, and I wasn't sure what I could do until Sr. Stella told me to push some of the people in wheelchairs around the yard. I did as she told me to. It was hard to tell if the person in the wheelchair enjoyed it. One of the men kept telling me something. I hoped it wasn't important because I didn't understand a single thing he said. I tried telling him that, but I'm not sure he heard me.

After about two walks, I got the hang of it and pushed five or six people in their wheelchairs. The staff members used gestures to show me what to do next, and they smiled at me a lot, so of course

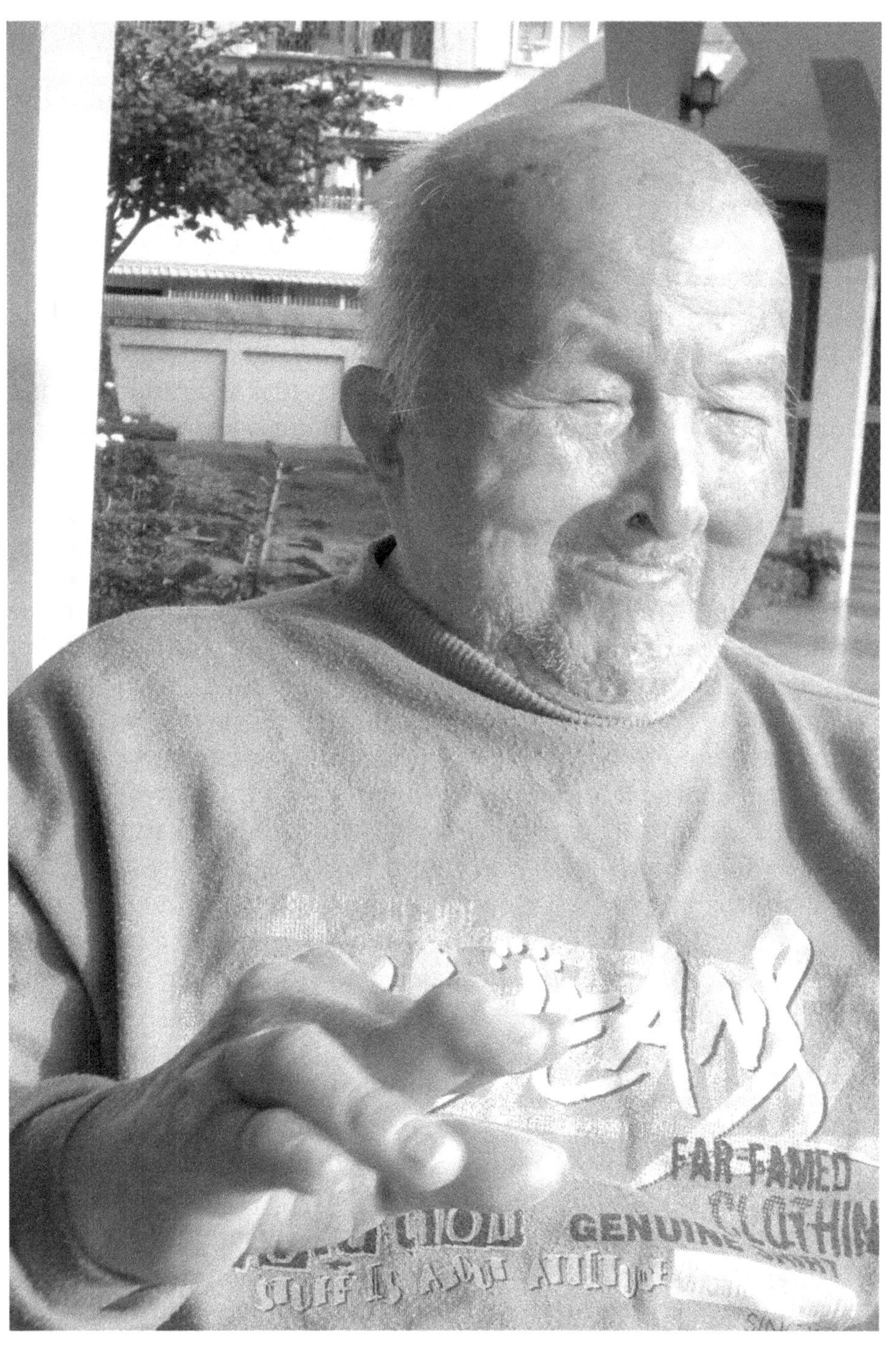

One man sitting in the sun looked like a Chinese Buddha.

I smiled back.

All that smiling made me wonder if a Barbie doll smile ever got tiring. I sure would wear out if I had to have that smile on my face every moment. Some of the old people I pushed were smiley and kind to me. When they look up and smile with their toothless, boney faces, I can't help smiling back. One old man kept trying to hold my hand whenever I passed. I let him, and he smiled at me every time. Another woman with winter-white hair also talked to me some, and she smiled whenever I passed. It became clear that I would end up preferring some of the older people to others because smiling at someone who smiles back is so much better than trying to communicate with someone who's mute, dull, or dismissive.

Looking at elderly faces all the time felt a bit weird at first, but then I started wondering how they looked when they were my age. I also wondered how I will look when I am their age.

One man sitting in the sun looked like a Chinese Buddha. I asked him if he wanted to go on a "walk" with me. He smiled and his face got rounder, but he declined. His Buddha smile was so cute, so I asked him another time just to see if he'd do the same thing, and he did.

Looking at elderly faces all the time felt a bit weird at first, but then I started wondering how they looked when they were my age. I also wondered how I will look when I am their age. I found myself hoping I don't end up in a place like this, though there are many caring people who help, and the facilities are nice. Still, I don't want to be in a house full of strangers and people younger than I in a place without those I love close to me.

Then it came to me that these people must be feeling similar things about being in a home for the elderly. Some of them didn't seem to be able to think anything at all, and I figured it must sometimes be a blessing to be forgetful, in spite of all the clowning the sisters do in teasing each other about being forgetful.

At the elevator when I was helping people go to dinner, I found another person I liked. It was easy to catch his eye, and he stared at me with open curiosity. When I turned his way or smiled, he laughed, and his whole face seemed to come alive with delight. I loved it, so I kept tilting my head or smiling at him. The man next to him in the wheelchair, though, was Mr. Grumpy Pants. I decided I liked the smiley-faced guy much better. But who knows, tomorrow Mr. Grumpy Pants might smile at me. Maybe he simply got tired of smiling like a Barbie doll would surely do if it were a real person.

I went to get my books from the fifth floor, and then went down to the basement where they feed those who need to be spoon-fed. Surprisingly, one of the helpers let me do some personal work, helping an old lady eat her hot cereal. I felt really useful then, but realized the helper might have an ulterior reason for assigning me to that particular woman, since she proved to be very, very slow at eating. She looked crabby the whole time and kept refusing the spoon I held. When she did accept a bite, it seemed to take her forever to swallow. The person next to her ate quite fast, but she had teeth and the woman I fed didn't. I felt sorry for one lady because the helper looked like she was forcing some rice down her throat. The distressed woman kept touching her wrinkled forehead and wincing. Unfortunately, just when the lady I was assigned to began to eat faster, Sr. Francesca pulled me away, saying it was time for me to go to my own dinner.

01/28

Folding laundry may sound boring, but in good company and with good music, anything can be fun.

This morning when I was working on my journal, my computer messed up when I clicked "save," resulting in my losing the whole shebang. This has happened to me before, but this time the amount lost was significant. Eight pages worth of writing!

Last time I lost something, it was a book report for school. I worked on it for weeks, and everything disappeared. I was too emotionally broken down to do anything. Today, however, I'm calmer. Sure, I am disappointed, but now I have a burning desire to write better than last time. So here I go again, remembering, rewriting what the computer tossed into the bit basket, then moving on to how my day is today.

I am now upgraded to folding the actual clothes of the residents and not just diapers. There are eighty people living in this facility, and for each one we usually wash an average of two shirts and a pair of pants and underwear everyday, so we have huge amounts of laundry to fold before lunch.

Folding laundry may sound boring, but in good company and with good music, anything can be fun. By now, I am pretty good at folding clothes, so I could probably work at a clothing store with ease. While folding, I realized that many of the elderly people now are wearing clothes that teenagers wear. Some are shocking pink, or bright green, and even ocean blue with some pretty designs. Maybe at one time people could tell the age of other people by their clothing, but not today. It seems to me some teenagers wear old ladies' clothes, and some old people wear a young person's clothes.

The fifth floor where I work takes in most volunteers because they need a lot of help during certain times of the day. To get in the building, workers must first check their own temperature for any possible illness they could bring in and get a name tag. Family members of the residents cannot go farther than the lobby because they could spread viruses or germs. So I have to check my temperature every morning. The thermometer used here is something I've never seen before in my life, though I've heard about it. It's shaped like a gun, and it's used like a gun, as well. The guard points it directly at my forehead and then shoots. After a few seconds, my accurate body temperature comes up on the screen where the safety device might be on a real gun. I think this is a good opportunity to find out my average body temperature accurately. I also want to "shoot" someone like that someday, but I think only the guards are allowed to do that.

Thus, I have my own tag which I have to put on every time I enter the building. It's one that's strapped around the neck like those you see officials wear for identification. It has a red strap and in Chinese it says "worker" instead of my name. I take pride in it. There are certain responsibilities that come with that tag, and after a few days of working, I'm beginning to know what I'm doing.

Sometimes people who have yellow straps instead of red straps come and help us on the fifth floor. By *us* I mean Sr. Annie, Sr. Paula, and two others who do the laundry—a man and a woman. The yellow-taggers, as I call them, are those who choose community service over going to jail for two years. They are usually arrested for petty things like shoplifting or drunk driving. Nothing big, nothing scary. This facility is one of the few that takes those workers in. Folding laundry might somehow help them build character. Anyway, I got to know two yellow-taggers.

The first one, whom I see more often than the other, is fifty-four years old. He has crooked teeth that are black and yellow and dirty. I might have seen a gold tooth in there, I'm not sure. He has a nice smile because everything on his face smiles, not just his mouth. He is tall and wears shabby clothing, which makes his potbelly more obvious. He has dark brown skin, and, judging from his odor, he smokes.

A lot of people stare at me here trying to guess where I'm from.

While I was sitting down at a table working to get the strings and dust off the Velcro of the diapers, he came to my table and put his elbows on it and stared at me. He was less than a meter away, so I could smell the smoke on him. All he did was look at me while I worked. I raised my eyes a couple of times because his stare made me uncomfortable. But even when I didn't look up, I knew he was looking at me. After a while, he asked me how old I was. I told him I was eighteen, and he told me he was fifty-four. Then he said that I was pretty. I told him in Chinese that my father is fifty-eight, trying to imply that "Hello! You're my dad's age, stop staring at me like that." But honestly, it was more of a curious stare, so I won't label him a creep. A lot of people stare at me here trying to guess where I'm from. One time I thought a Spanish priest was Filipino, and others here have thought I was Chinese, Vietnamese, and even Brazilian. Here I don't put on any makeup, so in a way I accept every guess as a compliment because they are commenting on how I actually look, not a face that's beautified and decorated with makeup.

Another yellow-tagger was much younger and had good taste in clothes. He turned out to be twenty-six, and he owns a music shop in Tainan. He said he plays the guitar for a living, and he was doing community service time because he got caught drunk driving. He said he had to finish seventy hours by March. I decided he was a procrastinator because he had started in September. He had long jet black hair, which gave off a greasy glow. He had a few strands of white hair, too.

Since I work on the fifth floor, I get much exercise going up and down stairs several times a day. Yesterday I did many stairs, so today my thighs are sore. I've been eating like a pig, so I need some exercise and the stairs help.

On Wednesday at two o'clock, Sr. Annie invited me to go along with her to another facility to shave men's faces as a work of charity. It took about fifteen minutes to go there, and while we walked she told me how things were twenty years ago. The facility was a combination of a home for the elderly and a mental ward. Today, she told me, it is owned by the government and businessmen. But twenty years ago, things were different. The Daughters of Charity came each week to this facility to help out. The facility was underfunded and run poorly on a day-by-day basis. Most of the old people spent their days and nights in a bed lying in their own bowel movements for the whole week, until the sisters came to help clean them up again.

The mental wards were once like jails, she said. Each was a big room with only one bathroom in the middle. People there were naked and dirty. Also, when someone was dying, the workers put a bowl of rice on a table next to their bed so that as long as they could reach the rice, they could live, and when they became too feeble to reach the rice, they'd die. The workers moved some of the dying people to a coffin while they were still alive.

From the outside, the building I saw was large and well kept. It was larger than the place where I work. I expected a modern hospital with white walls and attractive inside, but I was disappointed. In the entry it felt empty and quiet. We wrote our names on the visitors list and went up to the men's ward. The ward had about ten rooms, and each contained six beds for the patients. The place was a watery green color with gray and gave off a gloomy aura. One of the first men who greeted us was in a wheelchair, and his skin was browner than anyone I've seen in Taiwan. Sr. Annie said it was because he has liver cancer. He had a nice smile, too, and got shaved by Sr. Annie. Some of the patients were out and about, walking or pushing themselves in wheelchairs. But most were in their beds, under big covers.

When I first entered the room, the stench of the place hit me like a wall of dense air. It was the smell that everyone can recognize, but is difficult to describe. It was basically the smell of unwashed male bodies mixed with the odor of urine and dust. I found myself only breathing in half as much air as I usually do, so I became slightly lightheaded. Nevertheless, I didn't say a word and kept at the side of Sr. Annie as she greeted, blessed, and shaved the men sitting or lying in their beds. Most of them are bedridden and most likely have bedsores. Some of them did not have name tags on their beds.

"You made his day. You're probably the only new visitor he's had in years," Sr. Annie said.

"That's because they don't want their names to be known." Sr. Annie pointed to the blank ID's. "Many are charity cases, and so we don't know who and where they are from."

There were few workers, at least compared to the building where I work. They seem to interact with the patients only when changing their diapers or doing something medical like checking temperature or blood pressure. So, much of time these men are alone.

"Most of these people here don't have any visitors," Sr. Annie explained as we moved on to another room. All the men we greeted were very happy to see us and were polite and nice. Among the men we saw and shaved, there were two I got to speak Japanese with. One of them was seventy-six years old and still bright and sharp, just like Sr. Annie. He knew more Japanese than most people I've met in Taiwan. We had a decent conversation while he clipped his nails.

Another man was bedridden. He was older, but still aware of his surroundings, and I talked to him in Japanese. His eyes seemed dazed and looked above me, but he acknowledged me. After Sr.

The altar for a Catholic church in Tainan

Annie shaved him, I held his hand and told him to "keep healthy and well." He grasped my hand, smiled, and said thank you. He held my hand for a while, and I let him. He lifted his head from the pillow to see me clearly. As I let go and said my goodbyes, I saw that he kept his head up until I left the room, a sort of sign of respect, maybe. Either way, I was touched. It must have been hard for him to strain his neck that way.

"You made his day. You're probably the only new visitor he's had in years," Sr. Annie said, "and some of them have been here since I have—for over twenty years."

What a life, I thought. Twenty years in this place. I'd hate it.

After finishing the men's ward, we went to the women's ward, where Sr. Annie had her "boyfriend." He was the only man allowed into the women's ward. He was middle-aged, but had the mind of a five year old. He used to stay with the men in the men's ward, but they poked fun at him, so the sisters had to move him to the women's ward during the day and take him back to sleep in the men's ward at night. I could tell immediately that he was unique by his Santa hat and the look of innocence on his face. He had a pug-like face and thick eyebrows. He was in a wheelchair and was drooling a bit. He smiled to see Sr. Annie, but didn't acknowledge me.

She was so strong and heavy it took several men to drag her back into her ward. She was struggling and screaming.

The women's ward was gloomy and sick looking. It had washed out green, dirty yellow walls, and beige floors. Some of the women looked very young. We didn't stay long. When we were about to leave, we heard a huge commotion right outside. When we opened the door, we found four workers dragging a large woman in her forties. Apparently, she had tried to run away. She was so strong and heavy it took several men to drag her back into her ward. She was struggling and screaming, and she passed right in front of us.

"I think it's time for us to go now," Sr. Annie said, and we left without another word.

Beyond the walls of the mental ward, in the "fresh" air of the city, I resumed normal breathing. It felt as if someone had taken a heavy weight off my chest. We walked through quiet neighborhoods and parks. I guess I was still reeling from the heavy smells of the mental ward, because it was only when Sr. Annie commented that the area was once used as a garbage dump that I noticed the grime and faint unpleasant odors.

A huge dead rat lay in the gutter. I wondered how it died since its fur looked healthy enough, and it was fat, too. Probably poisoned. I asked why the cars parked along the street had covers over their tires. Sr. Annie said it was to save the tires from dog urine because that part of the city was plagued with so many stray dogs.

The next day I joined the rosary time again. This time there was a new member, a priest who had come back from Taipei after three days. When it was time to repeat his part of the prayer, he spoke in a clear, loud voice, taking a long time to say each word. The woman sitting next to him was the Franciscan nun who always sounded like she was mumbling the prayer fast, as if she wanted to get it over with. For each Hail Mary, and for each decade, the priest always finished last, while the nun rushed through the prayer. Thus the prayer always sounded messed up, and listening to them made me tense. I wondered why the nun wouldn't slow down for the older priest who obviously was incapable of talking fast. Didn't she realize that no matter how quickly she spat out her words the slow pace of the priest meant their prayer would last the same amount of time anyway? After so many years in the service of God, had she somehow missed the beauty of unity?

The priest occasionally glanced at the nun, no doubt I thought, in frustration over her quick babble. If I had not been so tense, I might have found it comical, for it seemed as if they might start a fight during the middle of prayer. But they didn't, of course. After the prayer finished, I saw them conversing normally, and I realized with a bit of silent embarrassment that I was the one distracted from the unity of prayer and that they were perfectly okay with their cacophonous style of speaking.

Today, my two favorite sisters, Sister Paula and Sister Annie, left for the Philippines. And in addition to losing eight pages of my writing, I also missed saying goodbye to them. I thought they were leaving later, and so I didn't go downstairs for a while. When I did come down, they had gone. I found out later that Sr. Paula wanted to say goodbye to me, but they were hurried into the car. I felt sad in part because I wanted to take a picture of Sr. Paula before she left since it was probably the last time I'd ever see her.

Because my two companions for the fifth floor left, I had all the clothes to myself and took until lunchtime to finish folding and putting them up. I'm going to be lonely again up on the fifth floor. Until Sr. Annie gets back, after a week in the Philippines, I will only have my iPod as my companion.

01/29

I cried myself to sleep last night. I didn't really seem to have a reason for my tears, at least I was too tired to think of one. I stayed up past midnight talking to friends on Skype. Now that I'm awake, I'm not sure why I was so emotional last night. It may have been because I missed my family and friends in Japan, but it was more than that. Although I miss them, I don't think about them much while I'm here. Living among the sisters is taking a break from being in Japan. I still feel like I'm missing a big part of this whole experience in Taiwan, but I can't put my finger on what I'm missing yet. Maybe my tears were a sign of my frustration and confusion.

My work here is quite limited; it is something anyone can do. These workers and caregivers have been getting along just fine with me not around. I'm just an extra hand, another face. Sometimes I feel out of place because everyone else knows what's going on around them except me. I think what I need now is acknowledgment and encouragement that I'm doing the right things, that my help is appreciated around here. Since I don't have that, I'm always uncertain. With company like Sr. Annie and Sr. Paula, I was able to avoid such thoughts by talking to

Even if I don't hear others telling me I'm doing a good job or my help is appreciated, I can continue, not for my sake, but for the older people here who do not have a long time to live.

them and helping them out with their daily work. Since they're gone, though, I need to fend for myself.

This morning though, I think I should consider my Shaolin teacher's words when he used the Japanese phrase that means the "unmoving heart." I can move through the day with inner peace, so even if I don't hear others telling me I'm doing a good job or my help is appreciated, I can continue, not for my sake, but for the older people here who do not have a long time to live. To make life a little bit easier for them is all I can do now. That might seem like a small thing, but it is not. I'm satisfied with that. Last night, I forgot that I am not working here for me, and I'm still enjoying my stay here.

But even if I slip out of the inner peace of the unmoving heart, the sisters here are always welcoming, and the elderly people's smiles are worth all my efforts. Maybe young girls like me are just too emotional. Surely I can set such emotions aside—those that made me have a meltdown last night—set them aside right now and start my day again.

I found out more about the hundred-year-old lady. She can walk! And she still wears panties, for she is one of the few who can still go to the bathroom on her own. She is the loudest in Mass when we give each other the sign of peace. She might say she loves peace, yet I heard that she is the one picking the most fights on the second floor. When she arrived at this facility, she always wanted to be the first in everything. She wanted to be the first to bathe, the first to go out, etc. She has obviously gotten better because I haven't seen any fussing from her. I can't help liking her though she doesn't really greet me or talk to me. For some reason, I admire her for being at once so old and so energetic and so picky.

Today there was more help around the laundry room: one woman and one yellow-tagged man I've seen before. He was not the musician or the one who stared at me; he looked like my dad when he was a bit overweight. This new man has a round face, shaved head, horn-rimmed glasses, thin eyes, and big cheeks. He wasn't tall, either, just like my dad. I could tell he got along well with everyone who worked there. He bought me a Coke after work was finished for the afternoon, and he tried explaining to me where to go in Tainan that is very historical. He also tried explaining the Taiwanese food

A student in the winter camp near Taichung

that's famous here in Tainan. I couldn't follow everything he said, so I just smiled, nodded, and told him I haven't really eaten much in the city. It seemed too great an effort to explain to him that I can't trust a lot of food here because I'm allergic to the two ingredients that go into most Tainan food: peanuts and soy.

Everyday, whenever I have free time, I visit the second floor where the more aware residents stay. I greet most of them, and they smile at me, many taking my hand. I like going there because I get enough positive energy, smiles, and compliments to last me the day, and I get to speak Japanese with a few ladies. It is also time well spent.

She has a loud but catchy laugh that carries throughout the whole floor. She's eighty-one years old but still beautiful by the standards of the young.

There's a woman I talk to everyday. She's the mother of Sister Stella. Her name is long and hard to pronounce, so I'll call her Magdalene. When I tried using her real name, she laughed and said no one has called her that since she was young. I like to make her laugh. She has a loud but catchy laugh that carries throughout the whole floor. She's eighty-one years old but still beautiful by the standards of the young. She doesn't have many wrinkles, and her gray hair has a lively sheen. She has been at this facility for a year now because of pain in her legs. She cannot walk because of this pain. Her unused legs are skinny now, just like those of most of the people who spend their lives in bed or in a chair. She has been diabetic for the past forty years.

Our afternoon talks have become habitual, so every time she sees me come into the second floor from the stairs, she waves at me to come sit for our chat. I try not to be partial, so I go to her slowly, greeting and asking how other people are doing until I reach the end of the floor where Magdalene sits everyday.

At first there was another older woman who joined in the conversation. She is eighty-nine and only has a few teeth, one of which is coated with silver. When she was young, she was a midwife. She said every month she helped about thirty births. She never married. Magdalene sometimes pokes fun at her for taking care of so many births and yet never giving birth herself.

"She didn't marry because she was rich and didn't need a man to support her," Magdalene said in a teasing tone.

"What's wrong with that?" the older woman snapped, speaking in perfect Japanese. It was a way of asserting her superiority because Magdalene lacked such fluency.

Conversations between Magdalene and me are patchy and sometimes confusing because while she understands Japanese, she speaks to me in a mixture of Chinese and Japanese. I understand most of what she is trying to say. At times when I do not understand, I nod, say nothing, and let her talk.

Magdalene is the eleventh child in her family. Her mother bore thirteen. Since they were poor, most of the daughters were given away at a young age. She was fortunate enough to remain in the family until she married at twenty-two. She had one child per year for the next four years. Magdalene has two daughters and two sons. Since her children were only one year apart, she could not take care of all of them, so–if I understood properly–Magdalene sent them to different "helpers" because they were too much for one woman to handle. She insisted that she did not give any of her daughters away, as her own mother had. She talked much about her children and her grandchildren.

Her mother's family is from the tribe of "Hakka" in Taiwan. They have their own language, and in the modern world, their own TV station. They look to me like other Taiwanese, though.

I was astonished to discover that there are so many different kinds of Chinese, even in the tiny island of Taiwan. Among them are Mandarin, Cantonese, Taiwanese, Hakka, and others. Many of the people living in Taiwan are thus bilingual from early childhood, though their multilingual abilities are useful only in a few, often isolated, places.

Her face was grim and stressed. Soon I saw her eyes turning red, and tears begin to spill down her cheeks.

One day when I visited Magdalene, she was on her cell phone with one of her sons in Taipei. I gestured to her, asking if I should leave. Immediately, she shook her head and pointed at a chair in front of her, and she gave me her crooked smile. I say "crooked," not because of the shape of her face, but because of her teeth. I think her teeth aren't really hers because they are too perfect, and yet it looks as if one third of them on the left side are missing completely.

As I sat down, I noticed her eyes were a bit wet. I thought perhaps she had yawned, bringing water to her eyes, so I paid little attention to her moist eyes. But right after she hung up the phone, I could tell she was not her usual happy self. She started talking very fast in Chinese. Her face was grim and stressed. Soon I saw her eyes turning red, and tears begin to spill down her cheeks. I cannot say exactly why she was crying or what she was trying to tell me in Chinese. All I know is that it was about her children and her suffering as a mother. I put my hand on her knee and listened to her. I didn't even consider asking her to explain it in Japanese; sometimes a woman has to talk with no interruptions. She told me she felt useless, that her legs hurt, that she cannot take care of herself, and she cannot even cook. Her children live far away, and even her daughter who lives right next door only visits once in a while because she has such a busy life. Magdalene specifically told me not to tell Sr. Stella about her suffering. I promised I would not.

I haven't seen Magdalene unhappy since this episode, and I'm glad of it. She is always glad to see me. I believe she looks forward to our visits, and so do I. She never leaves the second floor and has no visitors. I know she wants to talk with her daughter more, but Sr. Stella is a businesswoman, and, as Magdalene said, quite busy. When I first saw Sr. Stella, she gave me the impression of a relaxed jokester. But oh, how I was wrong.

Sr. Stella scares me now. She has asked me a couple of times to help her in the office. She's strict, concise, and demanding. She seems nice, but she's not, if that makes any sense. The documents she asked me to handle were important, but because I got them from Sr. Stella, the weight of the responsibility increased tenfold in my mind. During the day she is a serious woman and hardly smiles. I've seen Sr. Stella and Magdalene converse a bit—it was unemotional. Neither of them smile, and the conversation is quick. I feel sorry for the mom. Watching the tense exchange makes me appreciate how my mother and I relate, which is not quick or tense but consists of lots of laughs and much positive emotion.

After talking with Magdalene about less heavy matters, about the salaries of her relatives, and the bad economy of Taiwan, I went to help residents with a meal. I feel a bit more useful now that I know more about the routines of helping people eat.

The workers call it "feeding time," a term that startled me at first, for it seems to dehumanize the older people who need help. It made me think of a line in a poem where a king spoke in contempt of his people. "They horde and sleep and feed," he said. Feed. Like farm animals feed. But since all the workers used the term, I got used to calling it feeding time, though writing this makes me feel a bit guilty.

I am assigned now to the same woman who is always leaning on her right side. Her back must be deformed in some way. I've never seen her actually sit straight. She is eighty-seven years old, and her left eye is always closed. I've never seen her smile, perhaps because she has no teeth. She's a good eater compared to the others who constantly spill and spit out their food or take many minutes to swallow one spoonful. It didn't take long for me to get used to feeding her. Would it sound better if I wrote "giving her food"?

The only thing that is a problem occasionally is her posture. Since she is leaning, her face is also tilted to the right. Several times I was afraid she would choke. At one point she seemed to gag and her face turned red. I've killed her, I thought in panic, but before I had time to call for help, she let out a loud sneeze. It made me jump. Since then, every time she starts to look red I prepare for a sneeze or two. Thankfully, she's never sneezed anything out. I tried to help her itchy nose by wiping it with Kleenex, but that made it worse; she let out three sneezes in a row. I thought it might be my fault, but I said nothing.

At one point she seemed to gag and her face turned red. I've killed her, I thought in panic.

We all know how it is to have certain little bits of food that are hard to swallow. She has a lot of those moments, especially with bits of green onion or hard grains of rice. Since she cannot chew, she spits them out. "Spit" is not really the correct word here since she rounds her lips and blows out the difficult food on the tip of her tongue. The first day this didn't bother me because she was looking away from me when she did that. Today, though, she was facing me, and occasionally I had bits of food flying towards me. I laughed out loud, not from being amused, but from being startled and perhaps embarrassed for her or maybe for me since I winced and dodged.

All the people on that floor wear big colorful bibs for meals, and I learned to use the bib during a sneeze or when the toothless woman blew out some troublesome food. If anyone watched me, they would surely think it strange that I jerked the woman's bib up so often.

Feeding time finishes around 5:30, and after I helped the workers take all the people back to their own floors, I returned to my room and waited for dinner. Tonight is Friday, and we rented a movie that I will be watching with Sister Bertha, the only Filipino here since Sister Paula left. Thus concludes my second Friday in Tainan.

01/30

Since arriving in Taiwan, I've had several dreams in both English and Chinese. In my dream I understand people speaking Chinese, but upon awakening I never remember what they said. I've dreamt about people I've gotten to know here mixed in with my family and friends in Japan.

Last night's dream, though, was a pattern I've never experienced before. My dreams are usually about people I know, people I care about. This time my dream mixed the supernatural with the real.

I had a cell phone that contacted a demon. For some reason, I had an appointment with him, one I didn't want to keep. At first I was in a cathedral, and I was afraid to meet him. I was afraid of the phone, too, because that was the only way he could contact me. I tried destroying the phone, breaking it by pouring holy water into it, so the phone quit working.

But the demon, as a magical being, spoke directly to me through strangers I saw in the streets. They were perfectly normal looking people who paid no attention to me, then suddenly spoke weird words from the demon.

I came to a wooden circular table at dusk by an outdoor food stand. A tall, skinny man with black hair and a thin mustache sat in front of me. He looked like a musician, like a shy normal human being. Then a glow came into his eyes as a demon possessed him. The shyness went away; his posture became straighter and elegant, not grungy like the previous persona. Now the man looked confident, and had a very seductive and strong aura about him. His attitude towards me was as if he had known me for a long time, and almost lover-like, as if he had been wooing me for a long time. Then I woke up.

I did a Web search with Google on the meaning of dreams about demons. I don't remember the name of the devil. I knew it in my dream, but I forgot as soon as I woke up. The sites Google took me to said that the demon was something within myself. The information was too general and too distant, too impersonal, and I felt disappointed with the web sites.

Since it was a Saturday I didn't go to work on the fifth floor. I asked Chinese Sr. Francesca to take me out to Anping, an historical site near the place where we live. While walking around the temples, which are colorful and minutely decorated with tiny statues of men and dragons, I noticed that many people put tables with food and incense on them in front of their stores and homes. These are for the gods, Sr. Francesca explained. On every first of the month and every day of the full moon, many families offer food and incense to the gods. The food is varied. For every store, for every home, it is different. Usually, though, restaurants and food stands offer the food they sell, and families put out food they generally eat such as rice, noodles, and fruit. Some of the offerings are not items people eat. Some food had red ribbons on it, as did a pineapple on one table by a fruit stand. When I asked Sr. Francesca if we could buy the pineapple, she explained that the food tied in red ribbons was for the gods, and the gods only. Still, after making the offering, people do not throw the food away. After the gods take the spiritual essence

A martial artist exercising in front of a temple in Tainan

from the offering, what is left is the physical food, and people can then eat it.

I saw packages of cup noodles, or bread, and large bags of rice on the tables. The incense sticks, which are long and thin, have to be erect to burn properly, and a stick will burn for an hour or so. The odor is pleasant, a smell that reminds me of woods and temples. Incense sticks are usually brown. Some tables had a specific plate of ashes where people set their incense. Others poke the incense into the food they are offering. I saw several oranges and apples with three or four sticks of incense stabbed into them. It looked painful, though I know fruit cannot feel pain. Some cups of noodles had incense protruding from them. I figured the spiritual essence of the food might taste good for the gods, but it sure doesn't look appetizing to me with all those sticks protruding from it.

The money turned out to be a special kind of fake currency useful only for the dead or for ancestors in the next world.

In front of the offering table there is sometimes a large metal can. This can is usually dark with soot because people burn money in this can when someone in their family dies or if one of them wants to succeed. When Sr. Francesca first told me they burned money there, I almost said, "No wonder your economy is going down, given that people are always burning their money." But I kept silent, which was a good choice. The money turned out to be a special kind of fake currency useful only for the dead or for ancestors in the next world. The money is mustard colored, and the bills have a red stamp on them that says "luck" or "wealth" in Chinese characters.

I saw many fires burning today. Sometimes I saw ashes flying around the streets. Sr. Francesca said that the government asks people to stop burning so much so often because of the air pollution. But no one listens, and almost every house and every store has its large can for burning "money."

We went by taxi to Anping. It only took us ten minutes to get there. On the way back we walked a bit because we had chores to do, such as returning DVDs and ordering pizza for dinner. The sidewalks here are uneven, if you can call them sidewalks. There are constant ups and downs, so people must be alert to keep from falling.

While we walked, Sr. Francesca told me about her family. Her parents got married in mainland China and had their first son there. Unfortunately, her father married without the permission of his own mother, so there was much strife between the mother and the daughter-in-law given that all three generations lived in the same house in Taiwan. Sr. Francesca said she felt sorry for her mother, being treated so badly by her grandmother and abused verbally almost everyday. The children were treated well, though.

While we were on the subject of family and ancestry, Sr. Francesca said, "Every family has its secret." I wondered if that was true, and if so, what might my family's secret be?

When we were almost home, Sr. Francesca, as had all of the other sisters I've had deep conversations with, said she was impressed and surprised that my parents allowed such a young girl like me to come to another country by myself. "In Taiwan, you will never see that," Sr. Francesca said. "Parents like their children living with them and staying with them somctimes until they are in their twenties or thirties. They are so protective, and they will not allow any travel."

I tried to explain that as long as my parents know where I am and know I am with trustworthy company, they will let me travel since they believe I'm now old enough to take care of myself.

"You are," Sister Francesca said, "a very lucky girl to have such a variety of experiences at such a young age. I would like you to come back some day to teach our young generation about your experiences. Most of them here only study, and have no common sense. They need to be more open and have more general knowledge. I respect and admire what you are doing by coming here by yourself."

I was glad to hear that, though I honestly don't think I will be in a classroom situation where I'm the teacher. Currently I'm merely a sponge, taking in anything I see and retaining all kinds of experiences and language I pick up along the way.

01/31

I woke up a little later than usual—7:30. At my home in Japan that's still considered early, but now that I'm used to being half awake at 6:00 a.m., 7:30 is pushing it. Since it was a Sunday, Mass was at a different time, so I usually went out to another church with Sr. Elaine. Considering that I stayed up until midnight chatting with my friend in England, I was fairly alert in the morning. I wasn't hungry though, so I drank water and some sweet tea for breakfast. It was probably because of last night's pizza. I'm allergic to soy products, and the pizza most definitely contained something like soy oil. It made me feel sick to my stomach for a few hours, and now I just didn't have an appetite even though it was at least twelve hours since I had eaten.

It is impossible to explain the meaning of some Chinese terms in one English word.

Usually when I go out with Sr. Elaine, it's on a motorcycle. Today she said we were going by bicycle, so I was excited. I love riding bicycles, and it especially looks pleasant here in Tainan because you don't constantly have to go up and down steep slopes like I do in Japan. It's a flat land here, some parts were ocean a few decades ago.

We were going to the church where Sr. Bertha works. It is one of the largest congregations in Tainan, and the church building is large, too. It is shaped like a cross, very old-fashioned. Before we began our journey, the guards at the home for the elderly had to adjust my seat height, as the bike was for Sr. Francesca and Sr. Stella, who are much shorter than I. This took longer than I thought it would since the screw was very rusty. I felt *buhaoyisu* towards the man who was working hard. That is a Chinese word that means "embarrassed" or "sorry." However, in this culture it could mean many different emotions combined. It is impossible to explain the meaning of some Chinese terms in one English word.

Finally, after about ten minutes the screw came loose and they fixed my seat. Sr. Elaine was agitated by then because we were going to be late for Mass. At least, she thought we were. She was several meters ahead of me as she zoomed across the street. When I say "zoomed," it is an exaggeration. You cannot "zoom" anywhere in Tainan. It's too dangerous even to go slightly above the speed limit. Bicycles, cars, and motorcycles use the same lane and the same traffic lights, same turns. Though the bikes and motorcycles have their own section to wait in for red lights, they're usually spread out all over the street, mingling among the cars. I enjoyed the bicycle ride, though my father and mother would not be happy to hear about it. Even a slight wobble, a slight accident or bump in the road could throw me off balance or cause me to collide with the motorcycle next to me or behind me and mean serious injury or death. Thankfully, both ways of the journey proved safe, though Sr. Elaine strictly told me never to go out by myself on a bicycle because of the extreme danger.

I didn't realize what the Chinese reading was about until the last part where I recognized the sentence, "of these three, faith, hope, and love, the greatest of these is love."

At the church, Sister Bertha, who had gone earlier on foot, introduced me to many people who spoke Japanese. They were all patchy in their Japanese, like I am with Chinese, but they were glad to be able to try communicating with me and I with them.

The Mass consisted of more songs than I've heard sung in any other Mass. Most prayers were sung, and they were very long. Normally, if this were in English, I would be impatient, but with the songs in Chinese, I considered the overly long prayers an hour of study. I sang along well enough after listening to the chorus one or two times. Though I don't remember most of what I sang and I don't understand half of the words, I feel good knowing at least I sang in Chinese.

Of the readings of today's Mass I understood one because I had memorized that reading once a long time ago. It's the famous "love chapter" of the Bible in First Corinthians 1:13. I didn't realize what the Chinese reading was about until the last part where I recognized the sentence, "of these three, faith, hope, and love, the greatest of these is love."

Love is different from other emotions, for it is sometimes a matter of your will and your choice. Most emotions are unbalanced, insecure, and constantly changing. The power of the will to choose and remain dedicated to love should be forever, or so I tell myself. The truth is that I still do not understand so well this concept of love. Perhaps my confusion comes because we teenagers constantly refer to love as the "feeling" of warmth inside or the butterfly feeling you have around certain people. Such a concept of love though, is no doubt amateur and immature. I hope I'm beginning to understand the concept of true love. In the end it may be an act of will to love someone without envy, without jealousy, with no bad feelings, and with true unselfishness and warmth. But I still find myself speaking of love as a shifting emotion that is difficult to grasp and hold. And doesn't that set it beyond the control of the will?

After Mass, since we had a few hours until lunchtime, Sr. Elaine took me to a famous temple dedicated to Confucius. I realized when we arrived that I had been there before with Sister Francesca on one of my first days in Tainan. I didn't complain, though, because with different company I knew the experience would not be the same.

Sr. Elaine has many sides. She is a social butterfly, talking to many people and receiving many charitable gifts from parishioners. At the same time she is one of the most spiritually humble and honest people I've ever met. She is a comedian as well as a meditative person. Among all the personalities I've encountered, I think she has the most depth. She reminds me of my father, of his patient heart. She reminds me of my sister with her sneaky looks and jokes. She reminds me of monks with her desire for a poor and simple life. She reminds me of a child with her open and curious heart and mind in respecting other religions and beliefs.

In the temple of Confucius we joined a group of tourists and a guide who explained the significance of the characters and writings within the walls of the temple. I understood little, and I could not grasp the true essence of what the guide said even with Sister Elaine's patched-up English translation. What I did get from the tour was that Sister Elaine has a way with people, and she loves to seek understanding. I want to be more like her. When the guide spoke to us, she was so attentive and enthusiastic that the guide looked directly at her during most of his talk. It reminded me of my elementary classroom days when I concentrated on the teacher so much that she ended up looking at me more often than she did other students.

We both agreed that someday we will find someone to teach us the complicated but beautiful dance of old.

Since it was a Sunday, there were many more tourists and locals visiting this temple than when I went with Sr. Francesca. There were people doing a type of martial art, a slow meditative dance. Sister Francesca adored their form and concentration. I did too. We both agreed that someday we will find someone to teach us the complicated but beautiful dance of old. It is in this exercise that the body and soul unites, and meditation and calmness of the spirit come to the human mind. There is no better place than the doors of the temple to do this.

After our little excursion to the temple, Sister Elaine, who usually doesn't like eating out or buying anything superfluous because it is a waste of money, took me to a famous fruit store that has been there since 1947. I ordered an apple-pineapple fresh fruit juice. It was the best drink I've ever had. Elaine, who has to be the healthiest person I've met, ordered tofu and red beans for her snack.

I marveled that she chose tofu and red beans at a fruit store. Perhaps she goes overboard with her health issues sometimes. I found out later that Elaine has a type of disease that makes her age quicker than others, so she must follow a strict and healthy diet in order to keep her organs working properly. She has back problems as well. I am not quite sure what her illness is called, but apparently her body is almost twenty years older than her real age, which is fifty-three.

We rode home after the juice break, and boy, it was hot out. The full sun struck like a hammer and the wind was too sultry, so it felt like the hottest of summer days. The sun burned my face and arms.

Caroline by a temple in Taipei

On top of the heat there was the air pollution. Because of the exercise demanded by the bicycle, I breathed hard and had trouble with the thick air. I needed more oxygen. Since cars and motor cycles spew so many nasty hydrocarbons into the atmosphere, I felt almost suffocated and fought to breathe, gulping in the bad air. I wonder what my lungs look like now.

Lunch was simple: I had French bread with butter and some bacon. I talked with Sr. Francesca and Sr. Bertha, who were sitting at the round table with me. It was a good hour of fun conversation.

Sr. Francesca told me a few days ago that today I was going to meet one of the teachers who will later take me to the College Winter English Camp. We're to go this weekend. I was tired after the long exposure to the sun, and the lack of sleep was catching up to me, so I dreaded meeting the woman. She came with her five year old son around 1:15 in the afternoon, and I found the dread was ill-founded.

Twenty-eight years ago she was the first volunteer to ever come to this home for the elderly. She was a teenager then, and now she has a son, an adorable five-year-old. His hair was cropped short like most Asian children. He would have looked like an ordinary Asian boy if it weren't for his big, black eyes. They were very wide, round, and intensely black. He looked at everyone, and he charmed everyone. Within thirty minutes I found out much about this kid.

He loves chocolate and carries a stash of it inside his pocket, so much of it that his mom has to take it out for him when he goes to the bathroom because otherwise it will spill out on the floor when he pulls his pants down. He loves to eat french fries at McDonald's, and since the sisters' house is only three minutes away from the American restaurant, he calls Sister Francesca "Sister McDonald's." He wants to become a priest when he is older because he does not want to bother with marriage. He told me that he does not want to divorce or have any sort of trouble with the opposite sex. I smiled and thought you have no idea kid, you have no idea.

Furthermore, he is outgoing and loves to walk around by himself. At the same time, he is wise enough to speak politely at all times. He knows his age and size mean there are many places he should not try to go. I'm impressed with this little boy, and I think he may actually be a good priest someday, though his current motives are questionable.

After mother and son left for a late lunch at McDonald's, I took a nap then went to visit Magdalene. I told her I wouldn't be visiting the home on weekends, but I felt like I owed her a visit because I had to correct something I had told her earlier. I had said that her daughter would be coming home today, but I discovered it was tomorrow instead. I didn't want her to wonder and worry, so I decided to let her know.

She was happy to see me, and she said she had been eager for me to come because she had remembered a Japanese word she could not recollect from our last conversation. I was surprised that her Japanese is getting better every time I talk to her. I think her Japanese is slowly coming back since I'm speaking with her so much. We can communicate a little better now, and I'm glad of it.

Today she told me for the first time what she thought of my coming to Taiwan.

When I told her that her daughter was coming back tomorrow, she didn't seem to care. She said that Sr. Stella had been traveling all over the place for so many years that she, Magdalene, does not worry anymore. Today she told me for the first time what she thought of my coming to Taiwan. She said I was brave to come to another country by myself at only eighteen years old. She asked if my parents were worried because if she were my mother, she would be worried sick.

Her comments were another reminder of my parents' trust and generosity in allowing me to travel like this alone. Although I sometimes wish I were back home, I never regret coming to Taiwan. I have my down moments when I want to go home, but I know in my heart that I am going to stay here until the end of my trip as planned.

02/02

The past two days have been great. I felt useful, appreciated, and busy with jobs I know I do properly. Yesterday, because it was a Monday, there were many clothes to fold from the weekend due to a lack of workers. Because of that, I ended up folding over two hundred pieces of clothing during the morning. I felt accomplished, and even the laundryman was impressed.

I had my first Chinese lesson on *Popomofo*, a type of phonetic system in Chinese which all children learn in the first grade. It's the first step to pronounce and read the Chinese characters correctly. Most Chinese people study English through learning how specific words are pronounced. Thus many Chinese people have very good English accents because they know how to follow exactly the phonetic symbols.

I found *Popomofo* difficult. The sounds were familiar enough because I've been hearing them constantly for the past few weeks. But the symbols are ones I've never seen before in my life. Some were similar to the Japanese *katakana,* a type of alphabet, but the sounds corresponding with those symbols have nothing to do with Japanese, so I found the lesson confusing. The lady who taught me spoke some English, but she was mainly speaking to me in Chinese, which I did not understand for the most part. I did learn many new words though, and asked many questions. We strayed a couple of times from the topic (as usually happens during private lessons), and I learned the Chinese words for "player" and "womanizer." She told me I was a good student, and she is coming back tomorrow to teach me again.

Susan, an office worker I'm helping to learn Japanese, saw who my teacher was and asked me with a doubtful face if she was a good teacher. I said "yes." Susan wasn't impressed. She said that if I wanted to learn, I should ask Elaine since she used to be a school teacher. I told her I knew that, and I'd love to study with Elaine, but she is a busy woman, and I have no intention of making her schedule harder than it is.

Today I played ball with the elderly again. One of the men, who always wears a beige Stasy brand hat, threw balls randomly at some people who cannot catch well, so the ball would hit them. The man in the hat found this hilarious, and he laughed a lot and enjoyed teasing the other people who were bad at catch. I laughed with him a couple of times because he was one of those guys who just had a good sense of humor, and he didn't mean to harm anybody, though sometimes the ball hit places that could look like it hurt.

The seventy-year-old man who had excellent reflexes was there again, and we played ball together for the longest time. I think in the end we were both pretty tired out. Many people noticed our skill and were cheering us on. The others stopped playing ball to see which of us would drop the ball first because we were going at a pretty fast pace. Even at the age of seventy in a wheelchair, he managed to catch me off guard several times. Today I got to smile a lot, laugh a lot, and share moments of inside jokes with the older people. It was a good day.

I went down to the basement where the people on the fourth floor go every day to eat dinner. The lady I usually help with her meal had allergies really bad today. She had both of her eyes closed most of the time and was constantly pinching her nose or trying to sneeze. Her sneezes sounded like coughs. She spat out more food than usual today too, so I had to clean up some mess on her bib. When she spat things out, something got on my hand. I knew this was going to happen someday with her, and I didn't like it much, though I guess on my hand is better than in my hair.

His face became so hateful and mean that I think he doesn't deserve to be called the Buddha man anymore.

Also, I found out that the man who reminds me of the Buddha has a very foul temper. When one of the weaker old men accidentally bumped his wheelchair into the Buddha man's wheelchair, the Buddha man, in a split second, started kicking the other guy's wheelchair. I was shocked. His face became so hateful and mean that I think he doesn't deserve to be called the Buddha man anymore.

Tonight's dinner pattern for me was slightly different. I decided to start a habit of exercising thirty minutes on a treadmill in the home before going for dinner. Today I had my iPod with me, so I listened to music and watched an episode of a TV series my best friend downloaded to my iPod. It was a good thirty minutes, although by the end of it, I was dripping with sweat, so I showered before my meal instead of after.

I had a delicious dinner which Sr. Bertha cooked: bihun, chicken and veggies, and sautéed cabbage, and I worried about the calories. Sr. Bertha told me, "Food eaten with good company will not make you fat." I wish that were true!

Before going to bed, I'll write some about where I've been living with for the past two weeks.

I live in a large house, kind of like a dormitory, with many rooms and a big kitchen for everyone and a large dining table. I'm on the first floor in the guest room, where I have a personal bathroom. Upstairs where the sisters live they have shared toilets and showers.

I do my own laundry, help with dishes, and help clean up after everyone. Living with other people takes consideration. If one thought of herself only, it would be an unhappy house. There needs to be a balance of privacy and unselfishness, and courtesy is essential to maintain a peaceful atmosphere. We all help with the food, and we all clean up. None of us complains or crabs about whose turn it is to do chores, as sometimes happens in my family back in Japan. No one here assigns anyone jobs, we volunteer. We take turns with chores but there are no rules written in stone.

I think it's easy for me to live with people like this. I don't mind doing the dishes, knowing everyone else also does them. The sisters have taught me through their example that being unselfish and working together is the key to a happy home. If a person starts to be lonely, or starts eating and cleaning alone, our home would not be a home anymore, but a mere apartment with thin walls.

It seems to me that more teenagers could benefit from an experience such as my time with the Daughters of Charity. Many young people are spoiled by having no chores or duties. We have siblings, machines, and parents who help us avoid what we believe to be unpleasant chores. Saying "I have to study" is a common and effective way for kids to avoid helping out in the kitchen. But I believe some work would be good for teenagers. Chores are a part of life—these are responsibilities for an entire lifetime. Avoiding helping with the daily burdens of maintaining a household can breed bitterness and laziness. Those who learn to enjoy giving to others through sharing such work will find that it isn't a burden at all, but a part of shared living that is both meaningful and enjoyable. Maybe I can't go so far as Thich Nhat Hanh, the Buddhist monk who says we can find mindfulness and some sort of mystical meaning in washing dishes. It isn't *that* much fun to wash dishes, after all. But it isn't such a terrible thing to do.

02/03

From early in the morning I helped Sr. Stella with her paperwork. The job was simple: moving documents into better and more convenient files. She said I was the best person for the job because I could not read what was on the paper, and she didn't want anyone to read the documents. Great, now I wish I could secretly read Chinese well so I could discover the secrets in those documents. In my fortunate but annoying ignorance of Chinese, I completed the filing fast.

So instead of answering I said she scared me sometimes, maybe because she was a no-nonsense businesswoman.

The other day, Susan and other office workers asked if I liked Sr. Stella. They had a look that said, "We don't like her, what about you?" So instead of answering I said she scared me sometimes, maybe because she was a no-nonsense businesswoman. They nodded and said that they also did not like her. They said they all loved Sr. Elaine. I understood their sentiments, though I felt a little guilty for causing them to think I had spoken in agreement with them. Sr. Stella does come off pretty harsh and cold sometimes, and very businesslike. Indifferent, some may say. I see her at work and at home. She is pleasant to be around in the house where she laughs a lot, and her laughter is pleasant to the ear, like her mother's. She has slightly darker skin than Magdalene because her mother is from another tribe in Taiwan called *hakka*.

Caroline holding a friend's baby in a restaurant in Tainan

Because I went to the fifth floor later than usual, there was a huge pile of clothes to be folded. I stayed and finished my part by noon. Again I saw the musician. He said goodbye when he left for another city to perform with his guitar. Because he had a concert to do, he was dressed better than usual, and I told him he looked nice.

Today my Chinese language teacher came again, so I studied some before her arrival. The lesson was two hours like last time, and again we strayed from the topic. I feel like I learned much, but after she left, I felt irked not to be able to recollect every word we studied. I wish I had perfect memory.

I don't know his name, but every time I see him it makes me want to laugh because he looks like a huge bug.

Today was a busy day; I always had somewhere to go. I could chat with Magdalene only a couple of minutes. She has diabetes, and her sugar level was high yesterday. Today she seemed to be doing a little better. She thanked me for helping her daughter do her work, and she seemed saddened that I'm getting busy like her daughter. I haven't missed any weekday visiting her, though, and I don't plan to.

When it was time to help with a meal, I think my woman (the one I feed every night) actually smiled and laughed with me. Her mouth and eyes are hard to read because of so many wrinkles, but today I think I sensed a smile and recognition of me. It made my day. I never really expected that from her. I thought she was too out of it. She even had the courtesy to spit her food in another direction, turning her head away from me. I think I'm going to like her more.

There's one man who can still eat on his own, but he makes a huge mess every time. I don't know his name, but every time I see him it makes me want to laugh because he looks like a huge bug. His eyes are magnified with his thick lenses, and he always has his mouth hanging open. He has a thin, triangular face. Sadly, he never smiles.

Tomorrow I am off to another area in Taiwan for five days. I'm going to be staying at a university for a Winter English Camp. I hope people can speak really good English; otherwise I have a feeling I'm going to be left out, even if I'll be with people my age.

I'd like to note that by now my room smells like my room. I think I've been here enough to rub off my smell into that lonely little room. My shampoo and lotions provide a sweet and homey scent, so every time I opened the door I smell a bit of home. After I get back from my five days in Taichong, I will only have about two full weeks here in Tainan before I move on to another place, then return to Japan. I think I will miss this place, especially the sisters and the old people. Wherever I go in the future, I will never forget their smiles, their laughs, and their tears.

02/04

I honestly thought I wouldn't touch my journal today because I expected a normal night at someone else's home. But I forgot I was in another country. Different home, different rules, different culture.

After about two hours of driving, I arrived in a distant city. I slept most of the ride. The driver was the principal of a high school, and it was her students who would be attending the Winter Camp. Her English wasn't very good, so I'm glad I slept through the trip. I daydreamed about Japan, the future, and my so-far faceless Prince Charming, who's currently lost somewhere in time.

When we entered the town, the principal told me it was a poor town filled with farmers. Many rice fields dotted the town and there were few businesses, so it looked quite rural. In Japan, such a town would be surrounded by mountains, but here is all flat land. It reminded me of a desert, except for all the rice fields.

The principal's husband is a doctor, so their house is in the more fancy area. To me, though, her house still looked a bit dirty and poor. The homes were about three stories, and they were behind big gates which I suppose designated the area as upper class. A barking dog greeted us. It was chained to one of the houses closest to where we parked on the side of the street. The dog barked not at us but at a stray black dog that happened to be walking on the road. I soon discovered that the dog was chained to the principal's home.

Inside it reminds me of a Japanese home, at least with its size, but those who live here had a poor sense of organization. There was clutter all over the place, and no one paid much attention to home decoration. The dinner table was stacked high with dishes and books and papers, items that clearly had nothing to do with dinner. People took off their shoes to get into the house, but they had no specific place like a Japanese *Genkan* to put the shoes, so the boundary in the house between shoelessness and shoes was invisible. However, I took off my shoes as soon as I got in, just to make sure I wasn't breaching some mysterious etiquette. The family offered me slippers, but they weren't the fancy slippers I'm accustomed to in Japan, ones with cute decorations and warm lining. Those I put on looked exactly like the slippers the Japanese used to wear in public bathrooms—those brown plastic ugly ones. All family members wore such slippers inside the house.

I envied her all the space, but if it were my room, it would not appear to be in shambles.

I am staying in the room of the principal's thirteen year old daughter, Emily, who, like my own sister, is into Hannah Montana. Hannah was never my favorite character. Emily's room has wooden floors and is very large. The room is filled with rather nice wooden furniture. It could easily accommodate six or seven people sleeping on the floor. But it is also disorganized like the whole house. I envied her all the space, but if it were my room, it would not appear to be in shambles. She had several items my sister keeps in her room in Japan, such as Build-a-Bear dolls and teen magazines, but Emily's are scattered about. She has a gorgeous vanity with a large circular mirror made of very dark, rich wood. She doesn't have any posters. The walls are bare and white except one large portrait of herself when she was ten. She is the only child. I made a strong resolution that if I end up getting married, I'd want to have at least three kids, preferably four, in case I had an only child, a daughter, maybe, who was undisciplined and spoiled like the principal's daughter.

Before dinner I watched the movie *Angels and Demons*. At dinner there were several dishes on the table with vegetables and meat and pickles and soup. They kept telling me to sit down and relax, but I was agitated because I saw no plates! The girl, Emily, gave me a bowl of brown rice and that was it. I was confused, and I asked for a plate for all my other food. They gave me one but they didn't get one for themselves, which I thought was odd. I sat down, unsure what to do next. Eventually, they all got their small bowls of rice and sat down. We said grace and started getting food. I put my veggies and meat on the plate and took a mouthful of rice to eat with the meat because that's how I've been taught to eat. They, however, put the veggies and meat directly onto their rice, using the surface of the rice, so to speak, as their plates. So basically they ate their meal with little bits of rice and kept refilling the small bowl with veggies and side dishes until they finished the rice. It was a huge difference from the Japanese tradition of using many small, decorated plates for every type of dish. The meal was also quite different from what I'm accustomed to in America where we separate our servings on a single large plate. I guess the way that family eats is convenient enough, given that there were far fewer dishes to wash.

The father was a pretty nice-looking guy for his age. His face was round, but not chubby and he had large eyes filled with curiosity. He held no resemblance to his daughter except maybe his flat, wide nose. He must be a good doctor, whatever he does. He spoke the most English; second to him was Emily, who had been to America a couple of times already, including the NASA camp. The Mom, too busy a woman, I suppose, for extra study, didn't speak much English. After dinner I finished my movie. Then I went up to inquire if I could take a shower and where.

Emily's room also has a bathroom. At first glance there is just a toilet and a sink, so I thought the shower was somewhere else. When I asked about a bath, she pointed to her bathroom. I was confused because I saw no shower in there. I decided I'd just go in anyway, while expecting some secret entrance to appear, leading me to the shower. This is supposed to be a fancy house, right? I had high expectations.

But when I took a closer look, I saw the showerhead next to the sink, and below it there was a bucket. It seemed outrageous, for if I took a shower there on the floor, I'd get the whole bathroom wet, including the toilet and sink. I asked Emily stupidly if doing so was okay, and she said "yes."

Okay, I thought, that explains why this whole bathroom is covered in tile and there's a huge drain in the middle, and it explains why there are no carpets on the floor. I carefully put the change of clothes on the toilet seat, because that was the only possible surface I could put my clothes on without getting them soaked with dirty floor water and was far enough from the showerhead to keep them dry.

The whole bath seemed wrong, for there were no boundaries to separate me from the sink or the toilet. It seemed as if people could walk in anytime. I felt exposed and vulnerable, and I didn't like bathing in an open toilet room that people use daily. I thought about all the dirt gathering around my feet as a pool of water, dirt from those dirty and ugly house slippers. At least this was a girl's room, I thought. When boys use the toilet they are much messier, and they always splash urine on the floor or walls. I presume they do so without being aware of it. So it could be worse, I told myself. If Emily had not been an only child, she might have a brother and my bath could have me standing in really nasty water.

My head told me I was undergoing a bit of culture shock simply because this part of the Taiwanese culture, so foreign to me, didn't meet my own cultural expectations.

When I finished the shower I didn't feel clean enough. I hope when I go to an American university that I'll have better shower facilities.

My head told me I was undergoing a bit of culture shock simply because this part of the Taiwanese culture, so foreign to me, didn't meet my own cultural expectations. Still, I decided as I toweled myself dry, my Japanese clean-loving heart was surely forever scarred that night, and there would be many nights to come when I encountered showers and bathrooms below my expectations of cleanliness.

02/05

I woke up at 6:00 a.m. to go to school from the principal's house. The night before I wasn't able to sleep much, probably because they offered me English milk-tea at night and I accepted. Milk might be a soporific, but that tea contained a big hit of caffeine. Stupid me. In the end I fell asleep to the music of my iPod. I chose classical music to soothe the soul.

The towel I used last night wasn't dry yet. I regretted putting it into my bag with clean clothes. We didn't have time to eat breakfast at home, so the principal bought us a morning sandwich, which was two thin slices of white bread and a thin slice of bacon, egg, and some spicy onions. I knew this wouldn't last me until lunch, but I couldn't complain.

After a thirty-minute ride, we entered a more "modern" city. As we parked next to the gym, I saw teenagers flocking inside to the booth to register. I dreaded it. They were all either junior high or high school age, an awkward age in any country. Most of them glanced at me and then moved on. The principal's daughter wasn't much help to soothe my anxiety. Emily was too shy to begin with, and I had to keep asking her questions about what to do next. She wasn't helpful at all. She basically brought me to her mom, and her mom told me what I had to do.

I knew this was going to be a hellish weekend for me.

Unfortunately, I had to sit with the principal in the front row. The back would have been better so no one could stare at me so openly. I was obviously someone new and a foreigner to them. In the opening ceremony one of the teachers introduced me. It wasn't much of an introduction. The teacher just said that I was to join their camp, and I was to be an assistant English teacher. She asked me to raise my hand. The girl sitting right next to me kept smiling and trying to talk to me in English. She wore a garish, pink outfit, had thick, black hair, was quite chubby, and wore glasses. I could tell she was excited that someone new was sitting next to her. She spoke

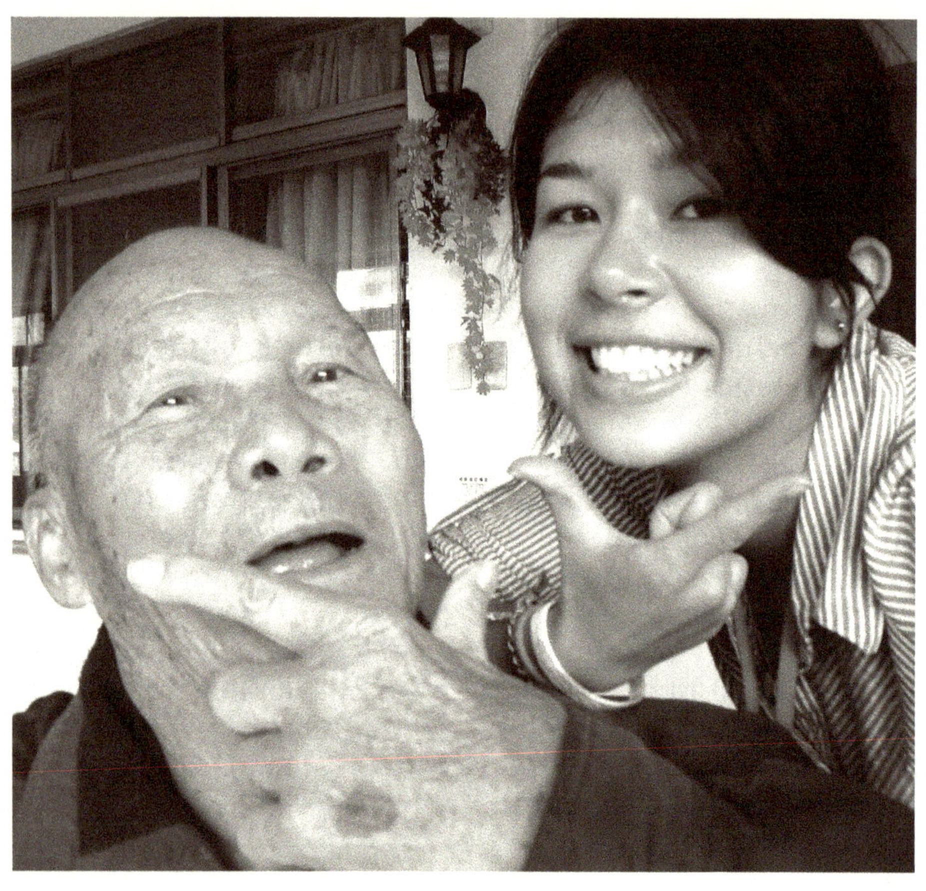

Caroline and her “boyfriend” who gave her lessons in Mandarin

pretty good English, and we managed to get ourselves semi-introduced before most students had to get on the bus to go to the university. I traveled with one of the English teachers in a car.

Most cars in Taiwan, except taxis, are horribly messy. My dad should never be allowed to spend time in Taiwan; he would die of stress to see so many messes and disorganized cars and homes. The ride took about an hour, and I slept through most of it.

My days at the university started out badly. I knew this was going to be a hellish weekend for me. The feeling that I didn't belong, didn't fit in, kept nagging at me. I shoved aside the bad feeling by joining in rock climbing, attacking the challenge with great energy, so I went higher than any of the girls. The summit of it was fourteen meters above the ground; I made it half way. Only two boys were able to go all the way to the top. At the seven-meter mark, my arms and legs shook with exhaustion and my hands slipped and my arms went limp, so the coaches lowered me to the ground. The chief coach gave me two thumbs up, and everyone cheered with me.

Despite such a victory, I felt unstable. If I had decided to let my emotions be in control today, I would be put into an asylum immediately. I wouldn't be violent, but I might be shouting and crying in frustration if I had slipped even a little in self-control. It was important to keep affirming that this camp would be over soon, for such thoughts kept me going.

I've had moments of total depression and utter loneliness before in Taiwan, but each time I've been able to assert swift control over those feelings. This time they lasted basically the whole day, though I was able to go on with what the day required. What hammered me was the feeling that I don't belong. I balanced that with the repeated affirmation that Taiwan is where I'm supposed to be for now.

I feel trapped, bound to the unwritten rules of a guest, and I am deaf to everything that is said to me in Chinese.

The school and students here remind me of Japanese students. They are from junior high to high school age and most of them are very shy. Those I talk to one-on-one can speak pretty good English. Each, like Emily, has an English name along with a Chinese name. I'm glad they do that, because otherwise I wouldn't be able to remember any of their names.

Although I am a "teacher," I'm really neither student nor teacher. I'm probably like what an exchange student feels like in her first day of school alone. All I can do is follow the teachers who speak English because then I know what I'm doing. Fortunately, several allowed me to tag along, and they helped a little in my need to fit in.

It's funny how I've been so eager to spend some time in this university, but now I can't wait to get out. I feel trapped, bound to the unwritten rules of a guest, and I am deaf to everything that is said to me in Chinese. This trip would have been one hundred percent different if one of my friends had been with me. But I know I need this experience. I don't know why I need it, I just do. It's one of those things I call destiny, and I think this thought helps keep me going everyday. I sometimes wish I were sick in bed rather than awake and thinking. But then, I like to think. I like to observe, and I like writing down thoughts and observations when I have the chance.

The sad truth is no one ever knows what the other is feeling. We have words, we have music, we have writing, but none of these truly captures and expresses what's inside.

First Day is over. Finally.

I watched *Wall-E* in Chinese at night, an experience that sort of helped me to calm my emotions, but stuck in a small room with tens of teenagers took its toll. The room reeked with the stench of unwashed adolescent bodies. The movie itself was in Chinese, so I'm glad *Wall-E* didn't have too many conversations.

I do not want to become indifferent or unemotional to everything around me because that's the point at which people totally snap. I am on the brink of it, though. I still struggle with negative emotions, and part of me suppresses them while the other part is trying to change attitudes from total depression to positive thinking.

It's not working. Not yet. I have moments of success, however.

Like my martial arts teacher once said, "Your smile is a key to success." For me it turned out to be "a smile is a key to happiness" or just "more smiles."

No one knows how I feel now, and no one ever will. Surely this feeling of isolation will leave a bitter taste in me for the rest of my life. I feel solitary and unique at the same time. Not even the closest person to me will know how I feel right now. How does that make me feel? The sad truth is no one ever knows what the other is feeling. We have words, we have music, we have writing, but none of these truly captures and expresses what's inside.

As this is a university, there are many sports clubs and athletes. While I was on campus, the university hosted basketball teams from Korea as well as other parts of Taiwan. I first was shocked at how tall Asian boys could be. They were over one hundred and ninety cm tall (six feet, two inches), some of them were shorter, and all were good players. One of them bumped into me, and when I turned to see who he was, I only saw the stomach of the athlete, and I had to look way up high to see his face. I wonder if being tall makes them feel superior or have some other effect. Most of the time, tall people I know in Asian countries wind up with a hunched back because they stoop in order not to appear so different. But these boys were tall and proud, though they all seemed lean and fragile looking, except for their legs which rippled with muscles.

Tonight, as I walked into an elevator going up to my dorm room with one of the English teachers, two handsome basketball players joined us. The teacher talked to them in Chinese as both of them started to eye me. At first I thought it was just me eyeing them, but it went both ways. I was curious about their nationality because they did not look Taiwanese. They were probably doing the same, trying to figure out where I was from. One was tall and looked half Asian and half American or European. The other looked almost Filipino; later I found that he was a Taiwanese aboriginal. He had dark brown, chocolate skin that was quite attractive. He had one piercing in his ear which gave him a look that I happen to find attractive. As they got out on the fourth floor, both smiled at me. I recognized that smile, one I haven't gotten in a long time, and it honestly made my day. That smile was one of those that openly said, "Wow. you're cute.

We should hang out sometime." I grinned. Some things are just universal.

We bumped into each other quite often after our first encounter in the elevator. I found out the tall guy's name is Hans. The other shorter, darker skinned one I found more attractive had a difficult name I can't remember. On our second meeting one openly said, "You are very cute," and the other asked my age. They are twenty-one years old and from Taipei, a big city in the north of Taiwan. These were stereotypical hot young boys who knew how to be successful with girls. I had my guard up since the first encounter because I knew they could be trouble if I let them. Thankfully, I was able to avoid or ignore every invitation to their room, as well as anywhere else. A girl can't worry about hurting guys' feelings when it comes to such flirtation because in the end she has to save herself. Such boys are hardly ever wounded, and they always seek other girls to hit on if they get rejected.

I returned to my dorm room, which almost felt like a cell to me.

To shift thoughts here entirely, I have heard about girls starting their monthly cycle at the same time if they are close friends. I sort of experienced that here. Not that I was actually emotionally close to the people around me. When I noticed that the girls I stayed with had their cycle, I was glad I didn't have mine, but it came quickly and in sync with theirs—a week or two earlier than it should have. Nature can be so irritating, sometimes.

I returned to my dorm room, which almost felt like a cell to me. It had a really ugly floor—a whitish color with black specks—and four desks with a bed on top. So I had to climb a ladder to go to sleep. It was like a bunk bed, but the lower part is a desk instead of a bed. Technically, there was no bed. There was just bare, white, hard surface without a mattress. I guessed the lack of mattresses was the reason we brought our own sleeping bags. Close to my room was a real horror of a shower, one that was worse than the shower at the principal's house. It was smack-dab against the toilet, and the tiles were filthy from all the coming and going of dirty shoes all day. Since I was the second person to take a shower, the floor was already soaked when I arrived. I carefully put my clothes where they wouldn't get wet, a tricky task since there was only one rack on top of the toilet.

In that moment I hated my life more than ever. I tried to shower away the feelings of disgust. It did occur to me then that most of what I was feeling that day—the mood swings and depression—were intensified by my hormones. But the shower truly was disgusting. As I blankly stared up at the shower while the water hit my face, I let a few tears slide out. Such crying didn't last, though, for I was too tired, too frustrated, and too upset to think further about my situation and pity myself. It is so weird to be too tired to cry.

I do not want pity from those who might read my journal. I would rather have anything than pity. If anyone has the energy to give me pity, I'd rather get sympathy. No words. Maybe a simple nod of deep and true understanding. That surely wouldn't take much energy, and to me it would feel good.

The sleeping bag was more comfortable than I thought, and I soon fell asleep after begging God to give me the strength and will to continue. That night I had a dream about my family, and I woke up with an uplifted heart, ready to start a new day.

02/06

It's almost scary how one day can be so different from another. Yesterday I was in mental hell; today I felt I could reach the sky. Even the horrible shower wasn't so horrible, and I got to make friends with many students. I prayed to God to help me understand Chinese. He gave me fourteen year olds who can speak great English and enjoyed helping me with Chinese. We went paintballing together, as well as partying at night with the student band. It was a night to remember. Our communication skills were not so good, but I felt we connected anyway. I have several groups of girls I go around and talk to now. I spent the whole day with my new friends. We played Hangman when we got bored, and we took a few pictures together.

The style of clothing and hair is plain and simple here. The girls remind me of Japanese students, but many struck me as boyish. One of the girls called the group "sissies." Many of them had very short hair, and glasses while wearing boy pants and boy shirts. One of these students, named "Apple" (yes, like the fruit), was one of my favorites. She couldn't speak much English, and when she tried to, she merely crammed random English words into a "sentence." I could tell immediately she was popular among her friends, and she was the comedian of her class. Every time our eyes met, we made a drama of calling out each other's name. For me it was easy, but it took a while for her to pronounce and remember my name. In the end, she just called me "Caroli" which is a Chinese version of my name. Maybe eating a lot of chocolate and drinking coffee today helped lift my spirits, but it was mainly the friendly atmosphere of the kids and their laughter and smiles that made the day so good.

I heard they were young and unable to speak much Chinese. I think I'll have something in common with them.

I have reason to hope tomorrow will be an even better day. English teachers arrive on campus from America. I heard they were young and unable to speak much Chinese. I think I'll have something in common with them.

02/07

The schedules here at the camp generally went thus: breakfast from 7:00 to 8:00; classes, lectures, or outdoor activities from 8:00 to noon; and more classes or outdoor activities until dinnertime at 6:00. On the first night we saw the movie *Wall-E* after dinner, the second night was a party, and today it was a performance by the students and the American teachers who came today. The theme of the whole camp and the lectures given by the leader of the American teachers was "Character Building." I think it is a good subject for teenagers who don't really have a Christian moral

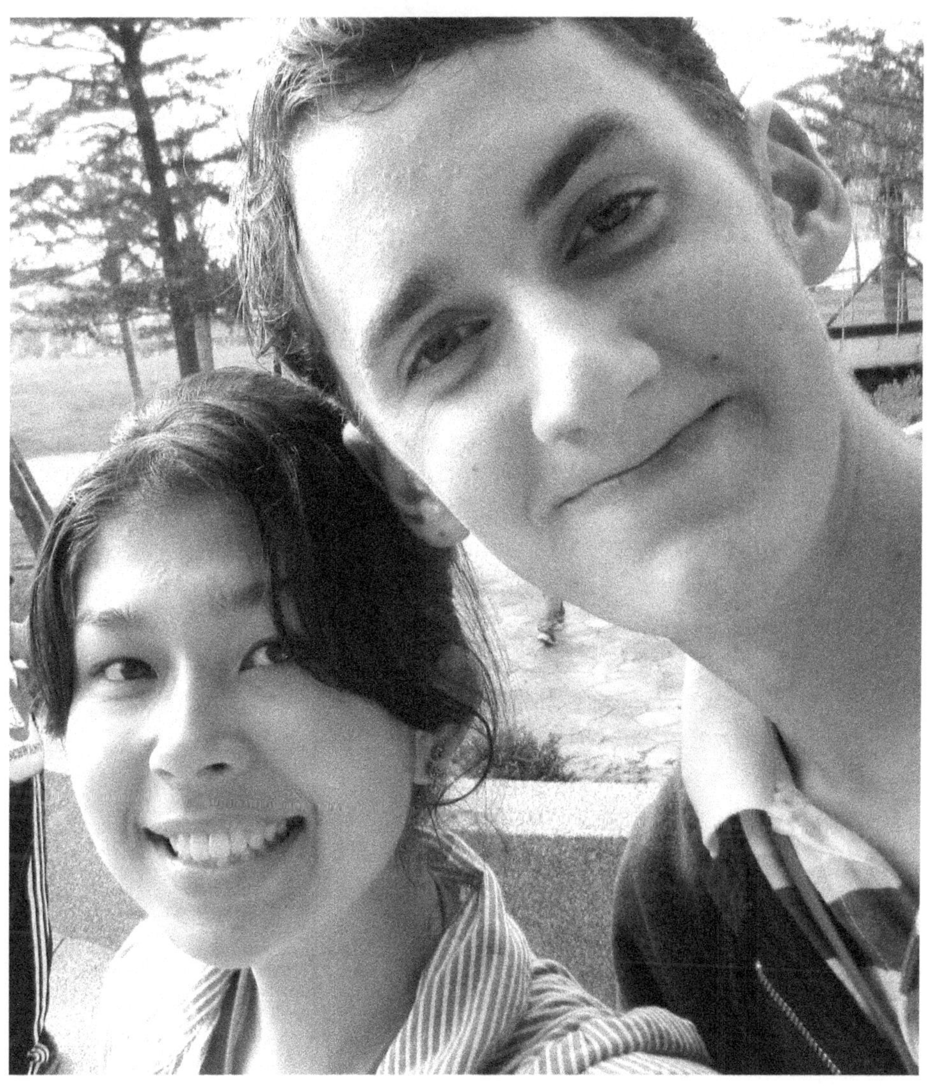

Caroline and a fellow teacher at the winter camp near Taichung

background. It taught the importance of truth, of modesty, and of obedience, and attentiveness. It was all common sense to me, but it's always good to be reminded. One of the lessons was about accepting who we are and learning to accept others. In this lesson the teacher taught that "unchangeables are not related to inward happiness"; in other words, that looks do not account for how happy a person can be. The text stated that "The assumption that attractive people are happier is untrue." I thought about it for a moment. Those who are unhappy because they are unattractive will in a way be happier if they are pretty because they are not struggling with their looks. However, being pretty also has its problems, and thus, you still won't be happy because you will still have some sort of problem. For example, here are problems attractive people face:

1. Exposure to more temptation
2. Deep doubts about their attractiveness
3. Resentment towards the motives of admirers
4. The fear of aging
5. Discouragement from comparison

I can relate to and understand most of these things. It is true about the deep doubts and resentment towards new friendships. It's more like a worry, and asking yourself "Why is he really talking to me?" I wonder if it's the same for boys. I sometimes think that good friends—one male and one female—are never just good friends. At one point or another, one will fall for the other. It may be for a moment or for a while, or even forever. Perhaps it's nature—and that's what I fear sometimes about friendships getting too deep, especially since I'm not now wanting a partner. I begin to doubt my ability to just be friends, and I begin to trust no one, not even myself.

As soon as I finished breakfast this morning, which was a hamburger that didn't taste good, the principal called me to join her to welcome one of the new American teachers. When I saw her from afar I thought she was much older than I, and I was sort of disappointed because I thought they told me that all of them were young. Plus, I only saw one foreigner, and I wondered where are the others? This new teacher and I got to be friends. I am so bad at judging the age of Americans. She has been here seven months, and she's with a teaching program. I forgot the name of it, but it was led by her boss, a bilingual tall Taiwanese man with glasses and very white, short hair. He looked to be in his late sixties, and he had a kind face. He spoke fluent English.

My new friend's name is Bertha, and she is from a family of fourteen brothers and sisters. She has copper hair and green eyes. She was the only one among the girls joining us later who wore any makeup. Maybe that's what made her look older.

As it turned out, all the new teachers are young, and there were seven of them: four girls and two boys and they joined in an hour or so later because their driver got lost getting to the university. They were a cheery bunch and all knew each other very well. The six who came later live together in the same dorm complex.

Bertha was the one who lived far from them and found it hard to fit in sometimes because everyone knew everyone else so well. I think she was glad to have me around, because I was also the odd one out. I also thought they were older than I, like in their mid-twenties. Turned out, though, that two of them were my age, and one was nineteen, while the rest were twenty-one, twenty-three, and twenty-four. The two boys were brothers, as I found out later. They were over six feet tall and very lean—so skinny and so tall—they looked like poles. They loved to play basketball, so they tried to talk to the Korean basketball players, who were even taller. When I first saw them, especially the girls, I thought they were Mormon or a very strict sect of Baptists because they were all wearing long skirts. I asked them, and they said they're non-denominational and they followed a dress code in their job that the white-haired Taiwanese man is handling. Of course, they can change to pants when they are doing activities, but when they travel and when they teach, they have to wear skirts. I wouldn't like such restrictions, but if the dress code was required by my program, I guess I would stop minding.

I'm amazed they have such steady jobs given that they do not have university degrees. All of them came to Taiwan right after they finished high school.

Most of them have come to the university several times. The boy my age has been here five months, while others have been in Taiwan for about two years. I'm amazed they have such steady jobs given that they do not have university degrees. All of them came to Taiwan right after they finished high school, and most of them had been homeschooled.

I was shy about talking at first, but soon I was able to open up and give them pretty good ideas. It pleased me that they were impressed with some of my ideas. I also realized that I won't completely fit into this English-speaking group because of my background. I was reminded again of my foreignness and wondered how I would feel in an American university. Brought up in an Asian country, but with some American culture as well as flawless English language, I am a unique combination, at least in Taiwan.

I noticed the Taiwanese English teachers were more extravagant and gregarious with the new English teachers. It almost seemed patronizing.

There are many like me where I live in Japan, but once I am out of my circle, there is no one like me. It feels as if people in Taiwan looked upon me as another species. Even out of the convent, I got complimented by total strangers sometimes—strangers like the lady from whom I bought my snacks. When I thanked her, she told me I was very pretty. I dread the day I start believing them and start acting like a stuck up witch. I hope that day never comes.

Anyway, the foreign teachers were very accepting, and they were glad to have someone to talk to using informal American English. They were bubbly and energetic, and their humor was odd to me. I didn't consider their humor very funny. They seemed quite innocent, and they often focused on one "funny" subject for a long time. They said the same thing in many different ways in their attempts to be funny. I often wasn't amused, but I laughed anyway.

I'd love to write more about my camp, but I think much of the experience is better remembered and treasured in my heart. Still, I would like to mention one particular issue concerning Asian culture: I noticed the Taiwanese English teachers were more extravagant and gregarious with the new English teachers. It almost seemed patronizing, and the fact that Americans got to stay in a hotel-like room while even the principal stayed in shabby student dorm rooms sort of explains the picture. Thankfully, the new teachers invited me to stay a night with them, so I got to sleep in a comfortable bed for one night. I slept like a baby. There were six of us in a two- or three-person room. One of the girls slept on the floor with my sleeping bag. I felt kind of bad taking her sleeping place, but they said she was used to sleeping on the floor, and she liked it because it was better for her back. I slept next to Bertha in a queen-sized bed.

The episode reminds me of Japanese society where hosts seem to try to impress foreigners with extra service and nice beds. In Japan, even normal sleeping conditions are usually nice, but in Taiwan I guess it's more understandable for the locals to make it easier for the foreigners who are used to more space and service. But what about me? I'm still not used to the Taiwanese baths and showers, and never will be!

One of the Taiwanese teachers, Tina, is constantly with us. Even when we go out of the dorm to buy a drink or take a walk, she gets worried about our getting lost, which is a silly worry. The campus is quite simple. No one can get lost because there is only one big road going in a circle with a huge lake in the middle, so even if you walk a while, the only thing that you accomplish is coming back to the same place after fifteen minutes. The English teachers felt too over-protected, and most found Tina a bit annoying. "How can we get lost here?" one girl said. "We're not stupid."

By the end of the day, we were all pretty comfortable with each other. I enjoyed their company and regretted leaving them that afternoon. Because it was the last day we spent together with the kids and teachers, both students and teachers expressed enthusiasm when I took out my camera to take last minute photos. I felt like a celebrity since I had been with the university students for four days instead of two (as were the American teachers). I felt that I got more requests to take pictures with the students than did the other foreign teachers. I was the local celebrity, being in at least one hundred photos. Half of them were with people I had not even talked with before the picture-taking.

We left the campus promptly at 3:33. I remember clearly because three is a positive number, and I was feeling good about the whole trip at that hour. What once had promised to be a hellish weekend turned out to be one of the highlights of my trip. I love how the world works, sometimes.

02/09

I slept in a heavy way, deep and dreamless, until my alarm went off at 6:35. Last night I returned "home" at about 11:00 and had to take a lukewarm shower because the heating system shuts down at 10:00 p.m. I unpacked mainly by throwing all my clothes in my dirty clothes section in the closet. So I have a lot of my own laundry to do today.

The one hundred year-old lady had trouble eating today.

It felt good to be back, and I got many warm greetings from all the sisters. I got the best one from Sr. Elaine, who gave me a big, long hug after Mass. I think I like her the most, though we don't always get to talk much because she is so busy.

The residents all recognized me as I sat down and acknowledged their welcome with a smile and a nod, and maybe a wave of a hand.

The one hundred year-old lady had trouble eating today. Maybe she had a cold or her throat was bothering her, but before Mass started she kept spitting on her tissue. At one point she put her hand in her mouth while making a huge gagging noise. I thought she was going to spit in her hands, but she just took out her teeth. I looked away every time she spat into her tissue. At least she didn't do that during Mass.

Today I got many emails from the teachers and students I had recently exchanged my email address and facebook with. I knew I'd never see them again, and I won't really talk to them, but I responded from courtesy. Lunch was simple: honey bread, egg, and yogurt. It was a lot of food. I took a two-hour nap until I had to wake up and get ready to go eat dinner. Today all the sisters are going out together to eat because Sr. Annie was selected to be the "boss" of their house for another three years, and Sr. Francesca was to be the boss for the new seminary. They called themselves "Sister Servant" or "SS."

While walking to the restaurant, I noticed more New Year decorations coming up. So much more red, and so many more wet floors. People clean a lot before New Year's, as they do in Japan. One has to be extra careful, because some of the wet floors are slippery, especially the ones made of slick stone instead of concrete.

There are many stray dogs in Taiwan. They are almost always stray, and very dirty. They are not shy at all around people, and they cross busy streets with ease. You see dogs running after motorcycles as well as riding on motorcycles with their owners. You see dogs walking on the sidewalk with people, see them eating any food they find. You see dogs just lying down in the sun, many pregnant with the next generation of strays. It is a myth that Taiwanese and Chinese people eat dogs. It may have been true during wars when people had nothing else to eat, like the Japanese who ate most of the squirrels in Japan during World War II because there was a shortage in food. These days there are plenty of dogs in Taiwan.

It is a myth that Taiwanese and Chinese people eat dogs.

Sr. Francesca is back now from the Philippines, and she is as talkative as ever. But now my companion in the house much of the time is Sr. Bertha. She doesn't work with me in the convent home. She goes out in the morning and comes back around 1:00. Tomorrow I resume working with the elderly, folding laundry and helping them eat. I hope some of them remember me, but I doubt they do because most people I greet everyday have dementia and can't even remember their children.

02/10

Today turned out to be one of my best days in Tainan so far. This morning I realized that we have four priests every morning to say Mass, though two of them are in wheelchairs. The

A priest taking Caroline on a tour of a church in Tainan

one hundred year-old lady came late, when we started to say the "Our Father." She was the loudest with her croaky voice. Two kinds of voices stand out and carry across the room, one is the cry of a child, and another is the speech of an old woman. I was half laughing while trying to say the "Our Father," not even hearing my own voice.

After breakfast I went out to do morning exercise with Elaine. The exercise lasted only twenty minutes, but the day was getting hot fast, and I was sweating already. The young musician came to work. He had a new haircut and was dressed well, as usual, and I got to talk to him more today. I found out that he has a beautiful girlfriend and that he will be spending most of his New Year holiday trying to put in his time for working as a volunteer at the home for the elderly. He has only another month to complete his community service hours. I wouldn't call him much of a companion, though, because he spends most of his time speaking Chinese with another man working in the laundry room.

The teacher taught me how to say "stupid pig" in Chinese. We laughed because we knew it was inappropriate language there in the formality of the sisters' house.

I feel left out, but as long as I have my radio I think folding laundry is an easy enough job. I sometimes feel that I could be doing more productive things, but then I usually realize that I'm actually helping many people by folding their laundry, and if I go down to "study" I'll probably just end up writing more in my journal, or chatting with my friends. Folding laundry is likely the most helpful way of spending my mornings.

I had another Chinese lesson today at 2:00 p.m. I was sleepy for some reason, though I slept well last night. I was only half awake during the first hour but woke up during the second. The teacher taught me how to say "stupid pig" in Chinese. We laughed because we knew it was inappropriate language there in the formality of the sisters' house. My teacher left at 4:00, as usual, and made plans for Friday when her daughter is to show me around Tainan.

I walked around the second floor to greet my old friends. To my surprise, they remembered me, and one man asked where I had been while away. Apparently he had also asked one of the sisters where I went, so I guess someone missed me. He said to bring a pencil and paper tomorrow at 2:00 and he would teach me some Chinese characters. I was excited until one of my friends from camp called to say that they will be dropping by tomorrow to take me out. I'm going to have to go to him in the morning to apologize, or see if we can do our lesson in the morning instead. I hope he's okay with it. I hate disappointing him, and last time I totally forgot about the lesson because I had to pack for the camp. It was the thought of him that almost made me unwilling to accept the invitation to go out tomorrow.

Three sisters came by today, one of them from the North. I had met her before when I was up in Taipei for a few days. Sr. Gloria Li is Chinese, and she came down to Tainan because her family lives here. She will be staying with us for about a week. The two other sisters visited only an hour or so from another community in Taiwan. One was an American from Louisiana, the other from the Philippines.

I really liked Jane, the sister from America. At first I didn't think there was any accent to her English, but by the end of her stay I could detect a slight Louisiana accent in her "theahs" for "there" and "heahs" for "here." She was a small lady with white hair and a slightly hunched back. She was shorter than Sr. Francesca, who was much shorter than I. What stood out most were her crystal blue eyes. Unlike Sr. Francesca—whose eye color is impossible to determine—Sr. Jane's eyes shone from far away in a brilliant sapphire. She is in her seventies, and those sapphire eyes are her most outstanding quality.

Dinner was amazing, and not just the food, for the company made it one hundred times better. I wasn't hungry since I just worked out on a treadmill and my stomach was still in its exercise mode, but I ate abundantly with the company and talked and laughed more than I ever had here. Elaine and I have several inside jokes going already, and I know Elaine enjoys them as much as I do. She's a busy woman and is often too stressed, so I hope that such fun and laughter helps ease her tension. It sure does for me.

Tonight will be a relaxed night. I already took my shower, and

I have many movies to watch, or I can choose to go up and chat with my friends. Oh, and tomorrow night is movie night for all the sisters, so I'm going to make them watch the movie *Up* about an old man and an Asian boy. I hope they enjoy it.

02/11

My mind is silent now. Too tired to think, I am letting my fingers do all the work. Today was not a great day, nor was it a horrible day. It was in between. It could have been a good day if I had not been so tired. I do not know why, but I kept yawning and I kept going blank in my mind. It is becoming easier to become blank, since most conversations are difficult to follow, and trying to understand takes much energy.

The truth is, I hoped they would not come. But they did.

Today I went out with people I met at the winter camp. Last night they called Sr. Annie to make sure it was okay to take me out. Back at the camp they had told me they would come visit me, but I did not think they were serious. The truth is, I hoped they would not come. But they did, and with some reluctance I went out with them. It gave me something to do other than to fold laundry.

But there was the old man who had told me to come at 2:00 for a lesson in Chinese characters. I went to him in the morning to tell him that I couldn't make it. He told me to come Friday morning instead. Later though, after I came back, Elaine told me the old man waited for me the whole afternoon. Apparently he forgot the change in plans. I felt guilty even though it wasn't my fault. I wish I had just stayed home.

The people from the Winter Camp took me to a fancy restaurant for lunch, the fanciest I've been to in Taiwan so far. The tables had forks and knives. The meal was a kind of European dish instead of the usual seafood and messy looking dishes swimming in assorted sauces. The company was nice, though it was hard to communicate because of my limited Chinese and their little English. The decor in the restaurant focused on aborigines of Taiwan. The room had odd-looking statues everywhere, and the whole building was made out of tree bark and glass. It was a beautiful place. Instead of a fancy table cloth, the tables were covered with paper painted with advertisements of other branches of the restaurant chain. After our meal we turned the table paper into drawing paper. We scribbled abundantly in Chinese characters, Japanese characters, English phrases, and some Spanish.

We went sightseeing after that. My stomach bothered me, probably from the food, so I did not want to walk around much. Even after I felt better, all I wanted to do was to go home to rest and talk with Elaine and Bertha or anyone who could speak English. It was too much strain to keep communicating in Chinese, although I had moments of laughter when they taught me a couple of off-color words in Chinese and Taiwanese.

We went to the beach just at sunset, so I took some good pictures. There were many couples there, and I felt a twinge of envy for the girls with dates. But the envy lifted when I wondered if those couples took notice of the beautiful sunset and ocean. It seems as if all they did was to gaze in each other's faces, totally in love. If I were on an ordinary date, would I be oblivious to the beauty of sky and ocean? The day when I look into the eyes of my lover instead of the eyes of the sun will, I suppose, be the day I'll know the man is the one I should spend my life with.

After the beach, the people from the Winter Camp took me back. I thought it would be a quick goodbye, that they would leave and go their own way, but they stayed for another hour talking and waiting for their other friend. Even when the friend came, they still kept at it, jabbering away in fast Chinese that made my head swim trying to keep up. It was tough to keep smiling and straining to understand when all I wanted to do was to go to my room and relax and eat dinner. They invited me to go out with them to the night market and to find another restaurant. I told them I was tired and I wasn't hungry, which was a half-truth, one that troubled me as I spoke.

But honestly, I just wanted them to leave. It's not that I didn't like them or didn't enjoy their company. I was tired, impatient, and strained to the limit with conversational Chinese. At that moment I realized an important trait I lack is a particular kind of patience. I can wait forever for things I don't care about —but for things that I do care about, I become impatient. Perhaps God is trying to teach me an important lesson in the grace of patience. If so, I don't want to admit it yet, since I'd have no choice but to try to learn a lesson that strikes me as quite difficult, and I'll have no excuses if I fail.

I thought the sisters' company would cheer me up and make me feel better. I was wrong.

Finally they left, and I went inside. I thought the sisters' company would cheer me up and make me feel better. I was wrong. I was still tired, still blank, and still on an emotional monotone. True, I laughed, but my heart wasn't really in it. I smiled, but it was superficial. I really wanted to watch a movie tonight with the sisters, as I've been planning for a while, but that got postponed, too. Patience, Caroline, patience.

It was summer weather today, so I was standing outside sweating horribly in my pants and shirt. At least I wasn't wearing long sleeves like those girls I saw at the beach. I do not understand their logic. Yes, it's supposedly winter and thus not a time for cooler clothing. But isn't the weather and the sun telling us it's a hot day, a day to set aside winter clothes?

Tomorrow I will have my Chinese lesson with the old man; we'll see how that goes. Then at two o'clock I will go out again with my other Chinese teacher's daughter. I hope I have enough energy to deal that much with studying Chinese. I really need it, but I feel like doing nothing. I don't even feel sleepy.

02/12

Its only 1:31 p.m. and I'm already sleepy. I have to go out at 2:00, but I don't know if I'm up to it, although I have no choice. When I told the sisters I had an appointment with the old man at eight o'clock, Sr. Annie said to hurry off right after breakfast because "boyfriend" would be waiting. And there he was, just as she said. Apparently he remembered that I told him I couldn't make it yesterday because he didn't mention how he had waited for me yesterday. He said he has been looking forward to teaching me this lifetime lesson for a long time. I was happy to hear it, and looking forward to it, too. I had no idea what he was going to teach me, or how. He told me to take him down to the first floor living area. There he told me to sit down, and he said that a woman would arrive at eight-thirty to write down all the characters he tells her because if he writes them down it would take hours, given the arthritis in his hands.

He also said that he is treating me like a granddaughter because he never had one of his own.

"Until she comes at eight-thirty, I thought it'll be nice to get to know you," he said. He also said that he is treating me like a granddaughter because he never had one of his own. I told him a bit about myself and my family, and then he told me about himself. He is eighty-two years old and received a strict Japanese education as a child, so at one point in his life he spoke only Japanese. He was a businessman who made a lot of money, though most of it had to go for medical expenses. He had a stroke at age forty-five, and since then has been paralyzed from his waist down. He said wheelchairs were not available until he was older, so he had much difficulty getting around. He was married at age twenty-seven to a beautiful woman. When his business took him south, he met this most beautiful woman and began a courtship. How romantic, I told him, and he laughed and agreed with me. It was easy to see that he was pretty proud of his wife's beauty because he mentioned it several times. She died eight years ago from stomach cancer.

Caroline having lunch with her tutor in Chinese

What he taught was an alphabet I was unfamiliar with, one he called the *bopomofo*, a term sometimes translated into English as the *Mandarin Phonetic Symbols*.

He mentioned that he was Christian, though not Catholic like the sisters. He said he was a devout Protestant. When I said his wife was probably waiting for him in heaven, he looked solemn and nodded. He's been at this home for six months, and before that he spent six months in a government-owned home, which I had visited a few weeks ago with Sr. Annie when we went as volunteers to shave the men. I told him he was better off here, and he agreed wholeheartedly. He said the home here is cleaner and had better food as well as better facilities and nicer people.

I was amazed at how much Japanese he could still speak and remember, and he can read Japanese characters. He recognized my name *Watanabe* and read it as a Japanese person would. So the thirty minutes of chatting passed by quickly enough. When one of the office ladies came to help write down what the old man dictated, we moved to another more private room and began work. What he taught was an alphabet I was unfamiliar with, one he called the *bopomofo*, a term sometimes translated into English as the *Mandarin Phonetic Symbols*. He used mnemonics to teach the alphabet, much like how children say "A for Apple, and B for Bee" and so on. But with the *bopomofo* there were several words for each sound. It took us about two hours, and there were over one hundred characters. I'm so impressed with his remembering the characters in order. While reviewing them, the office worker repeated each word in Chinese as the man translated it into Japanese, and I said it finally in English because the office worker was learning some English as well. How unusual all this is, I thought: three languages in one room with us conversing through a medium, this old man.

As the old man ate his morning snack, he told me to come to his hometown someday with my family. He said he will pay for lodgings, and he would love for us to be his guests. He was serious about the invitation, so I said the airplane tickets would probably be too expensive for all of us, and I wasn't sure what my parents would say to this idea.

The last time I said "okay" casually to people who said they would take me out, I thought they would not. Then they actually came for me. So I wasn't sure how to respond to his invitation. I know he has a good memory and is still strong enough to eat on his own as well as talk for hours.

As he ate his snack, it started to rain, a novel event, and rare. I've never seen it rain here. It was a most welcome rain because the region was going through a water shortage. During the rainy season, when the people in the region were supposed to get enough water to last them a year or two, the rains did not come. The sisters told me they are already preparing to save water. It would be horrible if the convent home, which relied everyday on washing machines to wash dirty diapers and clothes, ran out of water. Soon the government would issue an order to ration water. I hoped for more rain, but it stopped falling after only twenty minutes.

I love the sound of rain hitting the roofs.

02/13

Last night I fell asleep to the sound of rain. It was almost as though God had answered my wish for more rain. Two things in nature remind me of God. One is the lining in the clouds when a streak of sunlight spotlights a patch of earth. This reminds me of the story of Noah's ark, so I think of small hope in a seemingly hopeless situation and I feel the presence of God.

Heavy rain—especially at night—is a sound that comforts me in my darkest moods. Usually rain brings people down. Maybe a depressing rain is that which falls from gray clouds during the day. Last night my room was dark, and I had my window cracked, so rain hitting the roof echoed throughout my bedroom. It was a wonderful sound. When I am most in need of comfort or of a reminder of love, rain such as the one last night can allow me to go to sleep with a smile. I can get lost in its sound, in its beauty, in its cleansing, its strength and soothing rattle on the roof and windows. I would love to walk outside in the heavy rain and stand in the beauty of it until

I am dripping wet. An opportunity of that sort hasn't presented itself to me yet, however.

This morning more people were at the Mass because it is New Year's Eve. It doesn't sound weird to me—that February 13 should be New Year's Eve—though people in many parts of the world would find it odd. Tomorrow, in the lunar calendar of the Chinese, the Year of the Tiger will begin.

The hundred-year-old lady wasn't there to make everyone agitated. I wondered where she was. During the Peace sign, I didn't get the usual beaming "Peace be with you!" from Sr. Elaine because she was busy greeting everyone else, so I feel like part of the Peace will be missing for me today. She is leaving this morning to visit her sick father.

I wasn't sure how to use a mop, but I figured it out, I think.

As I brought the people back to their building, I greeted them with "Happy New Year!" and they smiled and waved. This is the first time I will celebrate New Year for a second time in the same year!

I decided today was cleaning day since my bathroom was getting kind of dirty, and my sink was disgusting with mold. My hair was all over the floor, too. Maybe my sister was right; I am going bald. I asked Sr. Annie for some cleaning material, for the proper chemicals, a rag, and an old-fashioned mop. I wasn't sure how to use a mop, but I figured it out, I think. I tried to get it done quickly so the sisters wouldn't correct me on using a mop, just in case I was wrong. I don't want that embarrassment. I felt like Cinderella, cleaning with a dirty gray mop and dirty water. All that cleaning made the whole atmosphere feel like fun. The chore wasn't so bad with a little imagination and music. After about ten minutes my bathroom and bedroom floors were wet, and I turned on the fan for faster drying. Sr. Bertha was just going out to the market, so I asked her if I could join. She said it was fine, so I had a good opportunity to take a walk and get away from my room while the floors dried.

Today is cool, a big change from a few days ago when it was like summer weather. I needed a jacket when I went out. It's probably about 17 or 18 degrees Celsius, compared to the 27 or 28 of the other day. Americans will find it odd that I use such low numbers for a "cool" day, but I'm accustomed to thinking in terms of Celsius instead of Fahrenheit.

Sr. Bertha talked much about people she knows, and she told me about many different buildings. I love to listen to her strong Filipino-accented English. When she goes to the market, she pulls a silver cart. I always wanted to pull the cart. It's something older people do all the time. I got my wish on the way back from the supermarket. She said in her clowning way, "What would your parents think if they saw you like this? Pulling a cart for the old sisters and doing so in such smelly markets!" I said they would be thankful to the sisters for training me.

Though the roads were dirtier than usual because of the rains last night, the marketplace was the same as usual. Such outdoor markets sell vegetables, clothes, jewelry, snacks, and other goods. This market stands on the side of a road where motorcycles always come and go, so the fumes are horrible, and since today is New Year's Eve, everyone is busy with last-minute shopping.

The indoor marketplace was a different story. Looking at the market, you might believe the vendors do not have the words "clean," or "organized" in their vocabulary. Places selling skinned whole chickens might be next to a place selling fresh fruit. Next to the fresh fruit might be more raw meat or even clothes. And next to the clothes you might find meat or fish. The stalls are so close together that some merchants are bound to have raw or cooked foods splashed on their wares. People were frying fish, cooking meat, as well as boiling seafood and cutting fruit all in the same area. Among them all was an abundance of clothing stores and shoe stores. The ground, always wet, had gutters running with dark red or brown liquid—no doubt mixtures of chicken blood, pig guts, and dirty water from washing the sea shells. I know I will never ever get used to shopping here, though I can understand how the market is normal to those who have lived nearby their entire lives.

By the time I got home, Elaine had left. I went up to check my email and stayed up in the office until lunchtime, and then talked via the World Wide Web to my best friend who now lives in Chicago. I plan to visit her in July.

Lunch was simple because dinner would be a big one—the feast of New Year's Eve. During lunch Sister Stella asked me to help at dinnertime because they were short of hands, as many people take off for the New Year holiday. I gladly said yes. I haven't helped the elderly with food in a long time.

After a brief nap I put on my volunteer tag and hurried to the basement where the people have dinner. They had just arrived, so I had to push a few people in wheelchairs to the washroom so they could wash their hands. The first guy I pushed directed me to the toilet, then to his seat, telling me what to do in sign language.

Today my job was a little increased. I put the bibs on the older people and helped seat them in their proper places. Afterwards I helped wash the bibs. As usual, I aided the old lady who spits out food. She kept eyeing me before I even had the food, so I think she knows I'm the one responsible for helping her. When I bowed my head and smiled as a sign of respect, she let out a loud noise which I take as a laugh. She's making a lot more noises like that since I began helping her. Though she cannot speak, we have a mutual thing going on, and I always smile when I think about it. She didn't sneeze as often, and she usually turned her head away when she spat food. She choked on the soup, but I've gotten used to that.

The people who almost live here, working everyday to earn money, see their life as routine. But for me, everything here is vivid, fresh.

I used to think of myself as someone in the way, someone who doesn't know what to do or how to help, as a burden, a heavier load for the real workers. Now I see myself as a proper helper, as well as being for some a refreshing and renewing influence. The nurses and caregivers seemed especially appreciative of my presence today, perhaps because they were short of people. They kept thanking me, and I kept smiling and saying, "You're welcome!"

Bottom line, I felt appreciated—a good feeling.

I also thought about how experience as a volunteer is good for the volunteer as well as the workers who do the work every single day. The people who almost live here, working everyday to earn money, see their life as routine. But for me, everything here is vivid, fresh—every spoonful of food I offer and every older person I push onto the elevator is a new feeling and new experience. There are a lot of smiles and connections the daily workers might be missing by seeing their jobs as routine and habitual. Having a volunteer around might help them realize that sometimes you have to pause in the routine to see life as new and fresh everyday. I know such mindfulness is almost impossible to ask of the hardworking nurses and ladies who dedicate their lives to caregiving, for I often see no smiles on their faces and a habitual hurriedness in their attitude. Maybe their appreciating me today was merely a result of its being New Year's Eve and everyone wanting to get their work done as soon as possible. Maybe not. It does seem clear to me today that being a volunteer and having a volunteer is good for regular workers and newcomers alike, even if the work is small and seemingly insignificant, especially at first.

The New Year's dinner was magnificent for the Chinese sisters, though I didn't find it that amazing. Yes, the food was good, but it's a kind of food I'm not used to. Still, the pineapple was the best I've tasted, and the desert was wonderful. I also had two glasses of champagne and one glass of sprite and wine mixed together. I had the drinks while eating, so the alcohol did not make my face so red. I had cheesecake for dessert. We had a good, fancy, and talkative dinner table, a fine time marred only by Sr. Elaine's absence. I hoped she was having a good time with her dad.

My second New Year this year went well. Like I said, I had a tiny bit of alcohol (legally, because the drinking age here is eighteen). In the solar New Year's day on January first, I was in the Philippines with a family I am close to. I didn't drink a drop of anything because I was getting on the plane to Japan the next day, and I was busy taking care of my friend who was, unfortunately, drunk. I think today made up for the relaxing fun time I missed in the opening of 2010.

Thirty minutes after eating, I walked on the treadmill and finished a movie on my iPod. I ran for about fifteen minutes and came back to my room dripping with sweat, feeling great about myself and cleansed even of the few drinks during dinner. Tomorrow

Students from the winter camp who visited Caroline in Tainan

there will be New Year's Mass, and then a rich lady will take all of us to lunch. We will be having many takeouts and eating out for the next week because the woman who usually cooks for us will be on a New Year's break from cooking.

I took a shower and felt refreshed. Sr. Annie is determined to stay up until midnight to see in the New Year, but I think I'll hit the sack after fulfilling a Skype phone appointment with a friend in England.

02/14

Happy Chinese New Year! This year on Valentine's Day. I wanted to go to Mass at a Church other than our chapel, but since we were going out at eleven o'clock to eat with some lady, I decided not to complain and to stay home like a good girl. The hundred-year-old lady spoke her "Our Father" fast enough to finish before everyone else in the chapel. I would think she would use her common sense at least on Sunday when there are more people, but I guess I can't say much, given that I'm a young girl and she's been praying for almost a century.

After Mass I went to greet everyone with "Happy New Year" in Chinese. It's a catchy and short phrase, and I feel happy just saying it. I brought my camera, and my "boyfriend" actually posed for me a couple of times. I took a video too, but all the elderly people weren't at their usual places that early in the morning. Magdalene waved to me from afar, and we talked for about ten minutes about her health and about the New Year, then I left her to help Sr. Annie with the laundry.

Each new year, parents, grandparents, and employers give gifts of red envelopes containing money.

During the New Year celebrations there is a tradition of the red envelopes. Each new year, parents, grandparents, and employers give gifts of red envelopes containing money. We have a similar tradition in Japan, but the envelopes are not set in a specific color and they are just called *otoshidama.* In Taiwan, the envelopes must be red. I've received three so far this New Year, all of them from the sisters, including one for volunteering to work on New Year's day. The money added up to 1600 NT which is about sixty-four dollars. I think I'll go shopping with that money, or maybe treat the sisters to dinner, if they'll let me.

At eleven o'clock, taking two cars, several of us went to lunch with a businesswoman who has helped the sisters here, especially one older Franciscan sister. Her name is Helen, which is my confirmation name. I've never managed to get her to smile until today. Since we're dining together, she became more familiar to me and even held my hand for support as she went down the stairs. She was a cute lady when she smiled, though at first I was startled because it was the first time I had seen her smile.

Lunch was a multi-course meal, all a treat from the businesswoman. Her company deals mostly with Japan, and she deals in hair decorations like barrettes and hair pins.

We ate some excellent Japanese food. I felt at home since the restaurant had good waiters who are trained to serve and treat you like a king. If this were in Japan, each meal would cost about 3000 to 5000 yen or 30 to 50 American dollars. Here it only cost 500NT which is about 1500 yen, or fifteen dollars. One of our waiters was a handsome Asian boy. He must have had some mixed blood because he looked different from all the others. Perhaps that's why I found him attractive. I have a natural tendency to spot people who are a mix of races like myself. He smiled at me, but then again, I was smiling at him first. I think I looked at him too much since I was trying to figure out where he came from. He was probably part aboriginal, but more like a quarter instead of half.

After lunch, we returned home and rested for about thirty minutes, then I went for a walk with Sr. Annie. She had told me about graveyards close by, maybe a fifteen minute walk from home, and I told her I was interested in seeing them. It seemed like a longer walk than fifteen minutes, and before we returned we had walked for almost three hours around Tainan city visiting department stores and borrowing DVDs for tonight.

When we turned right on one of the busy corners I saw that the tall buildings and the dirty looking apartments all disappeared at one point ahead. There was a large area where I could not see any tall buildings. And that's where the graveyard was, covering acres and acres of land.

These graves were nothing like any I've seen before. Each had a big area, an enclosure for the family to stand in and visit the grave. The graves were unlike the Japanese graves that are so close together or the organized American cemetery. These Chinese burial places struck me as quite disorganized. Much of the ground was black from mourners burning the tall weeds. Some areas with so much soot and low stones reminded me of photographs I've seen of cities that have been bombed. So much of the area reminded me of the rubble after a war.

The mourners leaving food believe the offerings go to their gods and ancestors. They also know homeless people will also eat the food. And that is okay, good, even.

The sky was white with clouds, and the pathway through the graves was narrow and sandy. A light scent of incense drifted through the air. I saw a couple of people visiting their graves and leaving food for offerings. Sr. Annie commented that there probably are many homeless people living in the graveyard because of the abundance of food from all the offerings. The mourners leaving food believe the offerings go to their gods and ancestors. They also know homeless people will also eat the food. And that is okay, good, even, for the spiritual elements of the food goes to gods and ancestors, so it is fitting that people who are hungry eat the remaining physical elements of the food. I think it's nice that something offered to the next world, or the gods, also serves to help the poorest of the poor.

For dinner, I had what I'd like to call "the last supper." I had a white *manto* which is a round, pure white steamed bread with nothing on it, and wine (mainly Sprite) for supper. It was delicious. I didn't want to eat more meat because I've had enough of all kinds of such protein in the past few days. Simple white bread with wine, and some chocolate for desert was the best treat.

Valentine's Day for me got a bit lost in all the New Year's celebrations, but then Valentine's Day annoys me most of the time. It always starts out good because I often get little things from people around me—sweets and maybe little stuffed toys—but in the end I always seem to be waiting for a special someone to say something to me, and I never hear it. So the day ends in bittersweetness. I know I'm not obsessed over it, and just because I didn't get what I want I'm not going to lie and say I had a bad day. I had a great day, so I don't care about the whole touchy Valentine's thing for now. But I do wish I had someone say "I miss you" or "I love you," someone other than family. But I can't ask for what only patience and time might bring me.

To have a foreigner, or someone different, or special, come into a house is an honor in Taiwan.

02/16

Yesterday I went shopping with the daughter of Mary, my temporary Chinese teacher. Mary was supposed to pick me up at eleven to bring me to her house for lunch, but she was late, as usual. According to Sr. Bertha, Chinese people are usually late because "any time is a good time." While I was waiting for Mary, Sr. Bertha told me how good it was for me to go to Mary's house because since her retirement, Mary has been pretty lonely. Sr. Bertha also said by having me, a foreigner as a guest, her rank or reputation will be higher in the eyes of her neighbors. To have a foreigner, or someone different, or special, come into a house is an honor in Taiwan. The same is true in Japan, also, for the Japanese love to have foreigners come visit, especially since such a visit provides a subject to brag about to neighbors.

Many people found Mary annoying because she talked a lot and because she has a strong persona. But I find her to be quite a nice lady. I love how she tries to speak English. She pronounces the word "maybe" as "membe" with the emphasis on the m's. Also, she cannot pronounce a "v" sound, so when she asked me, "How long will you wisit?" it took me a few minutes to understand.

Mary came at about quarter past eleven. She said she had awakened late, so she couldn't cook what she had told me she would, beef noodles. So instead she took me to the market and asked what I would like to eat. She introduced me to the market people, as they stared and asked where I was from. She explained proudly that my mother was American and that my father was Japanese.

I still can't get used to the marketplace, and when I saw how they treated the food I was supposed to eat, I didn't feel hungry anymore. The fish vendor handled his raw fish with his bare hands, then just simply wiped his hands on a towel to take care of the money. The fish lay on a table, all different types jumbled together. All the vendors touched with unclean hands the food they sold, even items we would eat without cooking.

Mary's house is tiny and disorganized as well as dirty looking, like every other house in Taiwan I've been to. It wasn't terribly dirty, but it wasn't clean. Her daughter, Jane, came to help her mom cook. I waited for about fifteen minutes watching TV as they prepared lunch. I offered to help but they told me to just watch TV.

After lunch Jane took me shopping on the streets where young people go. Immediately I found the slender pants I've been wanting since I got to Taiwan. I'm used to wearing baggy pants, and those that are boot cut. Since I've arrived in Taiwan though, I noticed young people mostly wear tighter fitting pants. I never thought I'd look good in them, but I tried them on, and they weren't so bad. They cost only fifteen U.S. dollars and looked to be of high quality. I bought five tops, and a pair of pants, as well as the cotton mask to help me breathe easier on motorcycle rides.

Unlike the difficulty I had with the acquaintances who came from afar to see me, I clicked with Jane, and though our understanding was patchy, we had a great time. I told her I would buy her a drink at Starbucks, a gift of thanks for taking me shopping and helping me become more stylish. While sitting at Starbucks, we managed some girl talk in spite of language difficulties. Being there was a real treat because it had been so long since I had found a decent Starbucks for hanging out.

We used notebooks to communicate difficult words in Chinese and in English. She taught me useful words and made up my Chinese name. It didn't take her long to come up with it. The first character, or the sirname, is *hong*, which has something to do with floods. Since my Japanese name also has to do with water, we thought this was appropriate. The last two characters, which are read *huimei*, are easier to explain. The first one is my actual middle name, and the last one means beauty. I really liked it, and when I returned to the convent, the sisters also liked it, though Elaine made fun of it as a joke.

Today I got special attention from the laundry man and several of the nurses because I had a bloody finger.

Jane is an independent girl. Mary taught her well about morality and independence. Maybe we got along so well because we have similar ideas about love, boys, and independence. She was really surprised when I told her the story behind my purity ring, and I could tell she wanted one, too. She didn't know such things existed. Within the two hours of our Starbucks chat, we probably covered many topics and laughed many times. I haven't had a decent hangout with teens since I was in Japan. Thank you Jane, for your time and help.

Today I am on the fifth floor alone since Sr. Annie is taking a retreat day. On retreat days the sisters stay in their rooms, meditating, or reading, or praying. It's also pretty cold today since it rained last night, so I'm wearing the boy jacket I bought yesterday. It's actually a man's jacket, but I don't care. It fits me, the color is navy, and besides, I'm a bit of a tomboy anyway.

It began to rain a bit while I folded laundry. I had my iPod with me, listening to music through earbuds, so I didn't realize it was raining until I looked at the window. I ran to tell the guy who's in charge of the laundry, but he said it was okay; he could dry the clothes he was washing in the dryer later.

Today I got special attention from the laundryman and several of the nurses because I had a bloody finger. It's not like I cut it by

Sharing an orange with a wild monkey near Taitung

accident or scratched it somewhere, it was just a result of extremely dry skin. I've had that cut for a few days now, but it was never bleeding. As I folded one of the shirts, I saw something red on my finger. Some of the blood had already hardened around the wound, so it looked worse than it actually was. I went to the laundry guy, and he freaked out. I told him it didn't hurt at all. He took me to the third floor where the nurse's headquarters are. When the nurses saw my bloody finger, they exclaimed such things as "oh poor thing, what happened?"

I didn't know how to say "dry skin" in Chinese, so I said I'll be fine and that it didn't hurt at all. The only thing I was worried about was blood getting on the shirts. One of the nurses took me aside and cleaned my cut and covered it with an adhesive bandage. The process took about five minutes. I went back to the fifth floor where all the workers kept telling me to be careful and watch out. The incident struck me as trivial and not something to worry about, though later I learned that some people have gotten deadly staph infections from simple cuts, and some lost a finger or a limb, and some have even died. From a cut on a finger! In my case, had I died, it would have been from a dry skin crack. That's hard to imagine, but I suppose it could happen.

She is among those who attend Mass every morning. She has white hair and tattooed eyebrows.

The rain beat down harder than ever. The laundry guy sighed much and said several times, "no sun today." He left all the laundry hanging out in the rain since it was already wet anyway. I finished folding the clothes around eleven, then having nothing left to do, I decided to go visit the second floor. I went to see my "boyfriend" first, and we made an appointment at two o'clock for our second date when he will review the words he has taught me.

One of the elderly ladies I greet always takes my hand and gives me a beautiful smile. She is among those who attend Mass every morning. She has white hair and tattooed eyebrows. Her hands feel warm compared to mine, and she always comments on how cold I seem. Usually I'm pretty warm, but today I was actually cold, and so

I agreed with her that my two layers of clothing weren't enough. Then I told her I was so young that I'll be okay. She laughed at that.

I didn't see Magdalene yesterday because when I went to see her in the morning, she was talking to her son's college friend and I didn't want to interrupt. Today she took me into her room to show me what he had brought her. It was a Chinese herbal drink for her diabetic problem. She said this helped her see clearer and feel better. *Chinese herbs* isn't the right term because the concoction she has is made from a part of a chicken, not herbs. At least that's what she said. It was probably herbs and chicken. She told me it didn't taste good at all and was smelly. I'm glad she has the "medicine" though, because she says it does help her, and she now complains less about having sore eyes and feeling ill.

She told me about her son who lives alone in her three-story house. Sr. Annie had told me a few days ago about one of Sr. Stella's brothers, who lived alone and had mental breakdowns often, especially around holidays because he was so lonely. When Magdalene started talking about her own son, her face distorted and she spoke more and more Chinese as her eyes got red and her tears flowed. I bent down and put my hand on her knees and listened to her. I understood most of what she was saying, though I can't express it here. She spoke not so much in Chinese as in the language of the heart, a language far beyond words.

She basically said that she wants to go back home to her son because her son is lonely and alone in the huge house. She does not want her son to feel left out, and she worries about him. She feels helpless in the convent home and she is homesick. Her daughter is too busy to visit her, and every time they get to talk, her daughter must rush away to work. "I don't know anything," is what Magdalene often says when it comes to her daughter, Sr. Stella. "She has her own work, and she is too busy to see me."

I gave her a paper napkin for her tears, and she thanked me. Our conversaton strayed from the gloomy to the happy, as she told me that it makes her very happy to see me everyday. I translated some Chinese words into Japanese for her, and she was delighted and commented that I have learned much Chinese since arrived in Taiwan. I'm not sure I have learned the language so much as become more open to new words and more willing to take chances by guessing their meaning, so I have learned to do better with conversation in Chinese.

I was happy to hear that she looks forward to our visits. I knew she did, but it was nice to hear it, and I told her I enjoyed our visits as well. She stressed again how her Japanese is poor because she wasn't allowed to speak it for the past sixty years after Japan left and mainland China took over Taiwan.

There was a minor race between the priest and the nun, but it wasn't as bad as I witnessed before because they were not sitting together this time.

We could have talked more, but the nurses called her to the table outside her room for lunch. I pushed her wheelchair to her place at the table, thanked her for a good time, and I left for my own lunch.

I found out something about one of my favorites of the elderly men. He's one of the younger old men, and he sits in the row in front of mine during Mass. He's the one with silver teeth who can still walk alone with a cane. I thought he could speak only Chinese, but I found out today he understands some of my Japanese. His name translated into English is Golden Dragon. What a strong name, I thought.

We were reading aloud some Chinese vocabulary I got from my "boyfriend" since he and I had a lesson today. We came to the word that means "queen," and I pointed at myself. Golden Dragon laughed and nodded with a childish sparkle in his eye.

I joined in the rosary for the first time in a while; for the past few days I have been preoccupied during rosary hour, which happens at three o'clock. At first I sat in the back, but another old man sat next to me and started to talk to me loudly in Chinese. I knew he meant no harm or disruption, but I kept trying to tell him to be quiet. It didn't really work because every time I opened my mouth to say something, he would say a dozen more words, so I just moved to the front where Sr. Annie led the rosary.

There was a minor race between the priest and the nun, but it wasn't as bad as I witnessed before because they were not sitting together this time.

After the rosary the elderly people always sing one hymn for Mary. I must say though, I don't really call it singing. It's more like groaning because most of them were off key. Anyway, I thought they finished the song when the Franciscan sister (Sr. Helen) began singing an entirely new song I've never heard before, in Latin. Her voice carried, though not in tune, and for a few minutes she sang with Sr. Annie a song no one there had ever heard. Such singing surprised me because I always thought Sr. Helen was a reserved quiet person. But not this afternoon. She smiled after she sang the song, and I went about my duty taking people to their places for another activity.

02/18

Yesterday was an eventful, fun, and informative day for me, so much so that I didn't have time to record all that impressed me. Well, Caroline, that's not entirely true. The fact is that I didn't have time because I stayed up until midnight talking to my friends.

In the morning, Sr. Annie informed me she would take me to TGI Friday's. I've always heard about the restaurant from my friends in America and England who have been to one of the chains and loved it, but there is no such place in Japan. When I saw a TGI Friday's close to one of the department stores, I promised myself that I would go before I leave. Sr. Annie knew my desire, and decided to take me. Of course, she liked to eat there, too.

The weather has been a bit odd the past few days. After we experienced summer heat, it suddenly cooled to the level of "very cold." For the South, this is very unusual weather, since the average temperature is between 18-25 (64-77 F). Now, its more like 10-18 (50-64 F). It's drizzling most of the time, and I miss the sun. I haven't brought much long sleeve clothing because I was told it was warm here, so I'm stuck just wearing layers and layers. I'm tempted to buy some more clothes, but that would make my load heavier when I leave Taiwan. I think I already bought so much new clothing that I'll have to consider giving away some clothes I brought from

Japan to make more space.

Before we left to go to the restaurant, I visited the second floor and my cheerful elderly people. I taught Golden Dragon to "high-five" me. So every time I see him, I raise my hand and he responds in the right way. We're awesome.

Magdalene gave me a mission today: she told me she wanted to speak to her busy daughter Sr. Stella about her son. I went immediately to Sr. Stella to convey the message. Sr. Stella told me she'd probably visit in the evening because it wasn't "urgent." I didn't say anything about urgency, but I had an idea she knew what her mom wanted to talk about. Back on the second floor I told Magdalene that her daughter would come in the evening. She thanked me, and I left for lunch feeling like an accomplished messenger.

It was sprinkling when we went outside beneath a gloomy white sky. Hate this weather. If it's going to rain, I want it to rain so hard I can hear the raindrops from the cozy indoors. Sprinkling is just a tease for me, an annoying kind of incompleteness that troubles me.

After a few minutes of walking, I saw a small dachshund running after a motorcycle. Wiener dogs are not cheap here, so it couldn't have been a stray or a street dog. It probably jumped off the motorcycle when the light turned red, and the owner didn't notice. The wiener dog didn't have a chance to catch the motorcycle, though its tiny legs moved fast enough to be a blur. It gave up after about a minute. I guess such little dogs have no stamina. It retraced its tracks, and I lost sight of the dog as I continued my conversation with Sr. Annie. A few minutes later, we heard a loud squeal as from pain or fright, and as we looked back, we saw a van stopped in the middle of the street. I think that was the last time anyone saw that dog alive, unless it somehow escaped death, maybe with some broken bones. I didn't hear any sound after the first loud squeal though. The scene troubled me, and I wondered if the owners would ever find the dog or even know its fate.

The scene troubled me, and I wondered if the owners would ever find the dog or even know its fate.

The yelp of the little wiener dog jolted me into pondering how fast life can change, but I couldn't give much time to that thought because of listening to Sr. Annie.

I've been bonding more with Sr. Annie. When we first visited, she had a bigger mouth than ears, but now she listens to what I say, so we hold enjoyable and mutually informative conversations. After we ate at TGI Friday's where I had some Mexican food (a rare treat in Taiwan), we talked about the fellow sisters we live with and their personality traits. I've wanted to discuss this before, to see if my discoveries and observation corresponding with those of Sr. Annie. They did, and I felt better about my ability to assess people.

One touching trait she has is that she knows her crabbiness is a flaw, but she cannot fix it.

Sr. Stella, as I've mentioned before, is a businesswoman. Most everyone in the care of the elderly fears her. Sr. Annie said she's tried to tell Sr. Stella that everyone is afraid of her, but Sr. Stella won't believe it.

Sr. Francesca and I think the way Sr. Stella asks for favors, though polite, sounds as if she is issuing commands or making demands. It's her unsmiling face as well as her quick movements that intimidates people. The problem with a leader inspiring fear, Sr. Annie said, "is that no one will tell you the truth."

I pointed out the fact that Sr. Stella is more mellow in the house, where she laughs much and smiles often. Sr. Annie agreed with everything I said about Sr. Stella.

Sr. Francesca has been more of a mystery to me than Sr. Stella. Sr. Francesca is hard to figure out because she seems to have no major flaws as well as no distinctive character traits. The only thing Sr. Annie admitted about herself is her tendency to being so vocal in complaining. She often has something negative to say. One touching trait she has is that she knows her crabbiness is a flaw, but she cannot fix it. Such changes take time I guess. Knowing your flaw is one thing, fixing it is another, but knowledge of a flaw is an important first step. I admire Sr. Francesca for her self-knowledge. Many people cannot see their own flaws at all.

One of the sisters with Caroline on a bridge near Taitung

Sr. Bertha is old-fashioned in rules and strictness. What I first noticed was that she never listens when the other sisters tell her to stop cooking so much food. She always cooks a meal for an army, and the sisters regard her as wasteful. She also cooks food the sisters prefer not to eat, like eggs and a lot of chicken. I love those two, so for a few days I ate chicken dishes and egg almost every meal. I think the cholesterol did something to my skin because I have worse acne now. I think I'd give up eating eggs for Lent if doing so were a proper way to regard Lent, which it is not.

Sr. Bertha and I visit well together because she is a listener as well as a talker. She is unlike Sr. Annie who has a big mouth and hardly gives me space to say anything. Apparently Sr. Bertha wants Sr. Annie to be stricter with the other sister's bad habits, such as being late for meals, not doing their housework properly, doing laundry poorly, and so on. Sr. Bertha wanted Sr. Annie to make more general rules in the home. I didn't know about Sr. Bertha's complaints until Sr. Annie told me. Sr. Bertha is also a night person, which explains why many leftovers in the refrigerator appear as by magic in the morning, items that had not been on the dinner menu the night before. Sr. Bertha used to be a tomboy and was at one time a skinny girl with a flat chest. Her penance was to eat three times as much as the other women in the seminary so she could grow stronger.

"Sr. Bertha has Parkinson's," Sr. Annie said. I was astounded, though I should have noticed the way her hands shook when she cooked or peeled fruit. "That's why she's not allowed to help with the pouring of drinks or with wafers during Mass. Her hands shake too much."

I didn't get to talk much about Sr. Elaine. I know she is a busy woman these days with so many responsibilities around the facility since a government official is coming to check up on them soon. If they are ranked one of the top ten in Taiwan, they will receive some money as reward, and if they get to be number one, they will have even more reward money, and they desperately need better funding. Sr. Elaine is a perfectionist and has so much work to do, but her tendency to get caught in many different conversations as well as her inability to use the computer well causes the work to bog down.

When I first came here, she laughed a lot, and for a while she and I had our moments of great fun and laughter over our inside jokes. But now, even if she sits right next to me for a meal, we hardly talk or even look at each other. She seems too engrossed in herself and her work, and when she does speak, she usually talks to Sr. Francesca or Sr. Stella in Chinese. She had told me she would take me to a movie, and take me to the church I liked this weekend, but she informed me later that she is too busy to do so.

Last time she smiled at me was a few nights ago when I gave her a hug for "stress relief." Sr. Bertha told me this about Sr. Elaine: "She does not know how to balance herself out yet. She is the youngest one in matter of vocation, and she is still learning the importance of balance."

I'm beginning to understand what Sr. Bertha said.

Sr. Annie told me about Sr. Gloria Li, who stayed with us a couple of days during Chinese New Year to visit her brother. I had met her in Taipei when I was up there for a few days. I've seen her many times, but it wasn't until today that I realized she was the one who invited me to come to Taiwan.

Her name and signature were on the copy of the official invitation letter I gave to the Taiwanese Visa office. The letter gave her title as Superior of the Daughters of Charity. Of course, I wanted to thank the Mother Superior for the invitation, but I had given up because I saw no one that fit the description of "Superior." I told Sr. Annie about my inability to figure out who held the title "Superior," and she looked quite pleased. She said it was one of St. Vincent's teachings that "If someone walks into the hall, they should not be able to point out the head of the community."

There was this one girl who went out at eleven at night to meet with some boys, and came back around two in the morning.

If I had pointed to anyone, it sure wouldn't have been Sr. Gloria Li.

Sr. Annie asked me if I thought she was the head of the house here when I first arrived. I told her I didn't know, though I suspected Sr. Stella was because she seemed to have the most authority.

Sr. Gloria Li is a quiet and reserved person. She has a kind smile and the look of a responsible and strong person. Sr. Annie told me a story once of Sr. Gloria Li's strictness in one of the episodes with some Filipino girls who worked for the home for the elderly. Currently there are girls from Vietnam who are volunteering to help the elderly. When I say "girls" here I don't mean girls my age, but women in their thirties. I call them "girls" because that's what all the sisters here call them since they are much younger than themselves.

Anyway, this story happened a long long time ago, before this home had been built. There was this one girl who went out at eleven at night to meet with some boys, and came back around two in the morning. At first, when it was her shift at night, she asked one of her friends to cover for her. The friend didn't mind at first, but these late night outings became more frequent, and the friend became tired of constantly covering for her. One day the friend told Sr. Gloria Li, the Directress at the time, about the late-night outings. Sr. Gloria Li immediately took the girl aside and told her that if she did not stop, she would be fired and deported. The girl, however, had no ears for such a warning. She went out three more times. The third time the friend called Sr. Gloria Li again. So Gloria Li sat on the windowsill where the girl always made her escape, and waited there until two in the morning for the girl to return. There she sat, waiting, and when the girl finally showed up, she told her to pack her things. Sr. Maria then drove her to the airport, and by breakfast time the girl was on the plane back to the Philippines.

Sr. Gloria Li, though appearing to be a soft-hearted person, knew exactly when to punish and when to be strict. I have much respect for her. The story about her handling the wayward Filipino girl reminded me of the importance of discipline.

I am now able to say all the rosary in Chinese if I have my book. I think I've memorized much, and I'm proud of it. When I first joined the rosary held in Chinese, my mouth never opened during the prayers, and my mind constantly drifted. Now I'm following every word, and I work at speaking the words in Chinese. My concentration on getting the Chinese right gives me no room to let my mind wander.

I had a decent semi-long conversation with Susan, one of the office workers whom I've helped with Japanese. The conversation was mainly about when I'm leaving, what I'm going to be doing, and when I'm going to a university, and I felt really good about myself because I was able to answer all her questions in Chinese.

There was nothing noteworthy until dinnertime when I went to help my friend with dinner. When I first began to help her and saw that she had a bad habit of spitting out some of her food with force, I knew a day would come when the food actually got on me.

That day arrived. I wasn't really paying attention to her chewing patterns and missed all the warnings of her "I'm ready to spit" face, and before I knew what was coming, I felt some food land on some of my face and hair. I wasn't disgusted, or repulsed, for it was just food from an old toothless lady's mouth. All I could do was laugh and think, "I had this coming." I also learned a new Taiwanese word for "eat." I knew the Mandarin version of it, but the Taiwanese one sounds more uplifting and catchy. It sounds like "jappon," whereas in Mandarin its "chifan."

02/19

Yesterday, through meeting one new person, I have decided on a course of study when I go to a university. Through a train of seemingly unconnected and coincidental events, I was able to talk to a sister who has a Ph.D. in psychology with an emphasis in transpersonal psychology and hypnosis. The topic of her career would have never come up if I hadn't mentioned I was somewhat interested in psychology. She then revealed to Sr. Annie and a priest who were there as guests, and to me some of her marvelous experiences helping troubled people, and she spoke in glowing terms of the almost magical effect of relaxation and hypnosis.

Everything she said fascinated me, especially her stories about helping people.

Everything she said fascinated me, especially her stories about helping people. I know I shouldn't make big decisions based on one person's accounts, but for some time I've wondered if I should study psychology. Of course I'll have to get a Ph.D. in psychology to really do something in the field, but I think I can earn that degree. My doctoral studies might not be exactly the same as the sister who works with hypnosis, but I would much like to start with psychology in a university. Just yesterday I wasn't sure of my direction and purpose. Today I feel like I've found them. Taiwan has brought many positive experiences into my life, but this one was different because it applied to my own near future.

How I actually met the sister who is a psychologist is a story in itself. I was about to go to lunch alone since Sr. Annie had gone ahead to visit with the guests (who was the psychologist's sister and the priest). I thought I wasn't invited, and that was okay. I went to the second floor to say hi to Magdalene and the old people and to make another appointment with my "boyfriend" for another Chinese lesson review. I talked to Magdalene a bit, and when I was about to leave, Sr. Annie entered the second floor to get a wheelchair for Sr. Helen since the guests were taking her out to MacD for lunch. I asked Sr. Annie if she needed some help, and she said to come along to meet these people.

I thought I was just going to push the wheelchair to MacD and help Sr. Helen get settled in, but it turns out that they invited me to have lunch with them at MacD. I really didn't want to, but if they were offering it was hard to say no, even having to face becoming semi-sick from eating the junk food because of the soy in it.

Right after I told the sister my order, Sr. Annie called me over and said Sr. Helen is going to throw up. It wasn't a surprise since she did that yesterday, too. I wondered if she had a virus, but couldn't think about that now. I went over to the counter and asked for a bag, but it was too late. She vomited on one of the empty trays. There wasn't much because she hadn't eaten anything yet, but it spilled on her clothes and some on the table. If I hadn't gotten over my fear of vomit and throwing up last winter, I probably would have become nauseated, and that would have ruined the rest of my afternoon. I helped to clean up the mess and was impressed with myself. I was even able to touch Sr. Helen and to escort her back to her room.

Because of this episode, we had to take our MacD lunch into our house, where in conversation, I found that the sister was an accomplished psychology teacher and counselor. It was from observing her kind, intelligent, and articulate ways that I found my goal for university study, for she is an inspiring role model.

Today was very cold. It's been cold for the past few days and I'm running out of long-sleeved clothes since my laundry doesn't get dry fast enough because of the damp weather. The weather is a horrible surprise. I came to Tainan thinking it would be like summer, but here it's as bad as the weather in Japan, and it's always raining. At least this rain might fill up the reservoirs so that the city won't have a shortage of water for a while. But the cold is unbelievably annoying. Sr. Annie said that this has never really happened before, and the weather is very odd this year. So is everything odd the year I arrive?

What started out as my helping a random person turned out to be someone I am very fond of now, though we have never conversed.

During lunch, I found out more about the lady I helped with her meal. She never talks, though she smiles and acknowledges my presence. She is always leaning to her right, as I've said before. Every person has a number with his or her name, and this number tells when they came to the home. For example, number one is the first person who came to this home. Now there are people whose numbers are in the three hundreds. My girl though, is one of the oldies—she's number eighty-seven. She's one of the people who has been with this home for the elderly the longest—seven years or more.

Sr. Francesca and Sr. Annie told me what she was like when she could still walk and push around her own wheelchair. Apparently she was a junk collector who randomly collected dirty as well as clean clothes of other folks to decorate her wheelchair. She always had plastic bags hanging from her wheelchair. So perhaps she had been a homeless person before entering the home. I've seen many such people in Japan walking around various cities. Obviously she was an odd one, this lady whom I help eat every night in silence. We have a connection now that even other nurses notice and smile about when I help her eat. What started as my helping a random person

A sister drinking a popular coffee bevcrage made with caramel and milk

turned out to be someone I am very fond of now, though we have never conversed. Maybe kindred spirits attract each other, not that I'm saying I would ever collect old people's clothes or hang plastic bags in my room. Today, while I was helping her eat, I noticed one of her earlobes had a large pierced hole in it. I touched it, and looked surprised and looked at her inquisitively; she nodded. She also opened both eyes today, so she looked better than usual.

I'm feel lucky to have this woman as my responsibility. Other women who need help with meals are very slow at eating. The nurses are sometimes forceful, putting large spoonfuls into their mouth, though having half of it spill out anyway. Today I saw a woman cough up her soup because the nurse was constantly pouring soup into her mouth without the old woman having time to swallow. Her head was in an awkward position already, so it must have been hard to swallow anything without choking. But the nurse didn't seem to care, and at least gave the appearance of knowing what she was doing. The woman, of course, continued to cough because she was half choking on the soup. After about a minute of coughing and reddening of the face, she was fine. I wouldn't do that to anyone even if I knew they'd be okay.

I noticed a change in the pattern of the people I bring up to the fourth floor for bedtime after dinner. I'm usually in charge of putting people in the elevator after their meals and pushing them out on the fourth floor where the nurses ready them for bed. I think I've mentioned before that the Buddha guy always likes to be the last one. Today though, he was the first, and it was obvious that he wanted to be first. I wondered what had changed his mind from being the last to being the first.

There are other odd people I tend to like though we seldom converse. One of the men looks like a witch.

Also, I had an unusual experience with the lady who constantly talks and touches her face. She almost always has her eyes closed, and she mumbles unintelligible words and sentences. She's the lady who was being choked by the soup. Anyway, she likes to touch her face for no reason. She keeps her hand over her face and uses her fingers to rub her forehead as if she is trying to rub away some kind of invisible disease. I wanted to see if she would stop this habit of hers, so while I was waiting for the elevator, I took her hand and slowly put it down to her lap. I held it strong, and she stopped her mumbling. Her hand didn't struggle against my touch and as I let go of it, it didn't go back up. There was silence on her lips and stillness in her hands. I thought she would start up again, but she didn't. Even when I pushed her in the elevator, she was silent. I almost thought she fell asleep.

There are other odd people I tend to like though we seldom converse. One of the men looks like a witch. He is one of the more aware and talkative men, who gives me instructions about where he's supposed to go when I am in charge of pushing his wheelchair. He has crooked teeth, beady eyes, and is bald. Plus, he has many birthmarks or maybe "sunmarks" on his head.

Mostly it is the women who react to my smile and attention, not the men. There's one guy who never smiles back at me, although, obviously, he's staring me in the face. Another man has his false teeth almost protruding from his mouth. I always wonder if his dentures might fall out while he is eating, but they never do. He doesn't smile, but when anyone passes by, he puts his palms together like in prayer and gives thanks to them. He reminds me of a rabbit for some reason.

I didn't get on the treadmill today after helping with the meal. I decided to take it easy today.

It was Friday and I left my jacket up on the fifth floor laundry room. Sr. Stella was supposed to come back today from visiting her family, but she wasn't back yet. During supper, we talked about Sr. Stella, saying things we would never say if she were around. I found out more interesting trivia about Sr. Stella that I thought was very cute. Apparently, Sr. Stella, who is fifty-eight years old, is terrified of the dark, especially the hall on the third floor. Whenever she goes up there, she asks one of the sisters to accompany her. When she was a bit younger, she asked sisters to come outside with her at night when she forgot to take her laundry down during the day. She's so afraid to go anywhere at night that she always has to have someone to accompany her if she goes outside. She also has a tendency to lock doors at night, a habit that has caused several of us to be locked out of the house early in the evening.

She is also terrified of the dead and the sick. I thought this was odd because I heard that she had worked with the AIDS patients. The sisters corrected me saying that she worked as an administrator and office worker. For some reason, I was a bit disappointed to hear of her fears. Apparently, she cannot bear touching a dead person, so when the sisters have to clean a body, she keeps her hands to herself. Such a response is understandable I guess, but Sr. Francesca told me of one of the episodes with Sr. Stella which shocked me.

Apparently, she cannot bear touching a dead person, so when the sisters have to clean a body, she keeps her hands to herself.

One day as she ate lunch with Sr. Francesca, her phone rang and her sister told Sr. Stella that her father was on his death bed. Sr. Stella said that she would go "tomorrow." Sr. Francesca immediately said, "No, you have to go today. Your father is dying, for goodness sake." Under such pressure Sr. Stella went to her father, and he passed away that day. If Sr. Francesca hadn't been there to knock some sense into Sr. Stella, she would have never seen her father alive again.

I wonder about the workers who think of Sr. Stella as some sort of witch; would they feel pity for her if they knew about her vulnerabilities? And I wonder why she is so fearful of the dark, about the traumas that must be behind such behavior. But like many disquieting mysteries in life, I shall never find out.

02/21

Where to start? Yesterday I visited a friend I know through a close friend who lives in Japan. How we met and how we got together are not important. The fact is that a foreigner would take me around Taiwan for a change, one who is not a sister. We went to Haian road, which is the center for young people's styles and exotic “good” food. But, of course, exotic foods can be dangerous, given my allergies.

Steve and Lizzy took me out. Steve is South African and Lizzy is Taiwanese. They have been living together in a small, cozy house in the suburbs of Tainan city. Anyway, I had only my small green tea frappachino fix for lunch, so when we went to visit the food markets, I was a bit impatient to eat something. It was already three o’clock or four. Lizzy took all of us to a famous local place where food vendors sell bowls of meat and rice. It’s not a restaurant, but one of those places where people eat outside, and it’s kind of dirty. I didn’t mind because I had good company. The meat and rice tasted good, but I had a strange feeling from my first bite that I was not right with it. Was it my sixth sense telling me that there’s something I’m allergic to in the food? But I couldn’t taste it. I asked Steve to ask the food vendors if they had cooked with soy or peanuts, and they said no. So I continued to eat. My mouth felt a bit cottony, but I ate anyway, knowing I would feel bad leaving food Steve and Lizzy had bought for me. Besides, I thought I could handle an allergic reaction. But I was dead wrong.

Besides, I thought I could handle an allergic reaction. But I was dead wrong.

Immediately after I finished the bowl I began to feel sick at the stomach. It wasn’t anything I’ve experienced before with any of my allergies. Usually with soy products, if it isn’t the hardcore protein, I get away with a slight itch of the throat or swollen lips. If it’s peanuts, I might die. If it was peanut oil, or something of that sort, I’d probably throw up or get a really bad stomachache. But I haven’t tried enough foods to really know exactly what happens, and I hope I never find out. This stomachache though, was an odd one. I felt limp and hot like I had some fever. Then again, I was sitting in the sun. It became hard to concentrate, and I lost track of what Steve and Lizzy were talking about. I tried to participate in order to take my mind off the thought that kept nagging at me: Caroline, you’re having an allergic reaction. Am I going to throw up? I wondered. Am I going to faint?

I told Lizzy and Steve I wasn't feeling great, and I smiled and told them I'd probably feel better with a yogurt drink. Steve asked me if on a scale of 1 to 10 how I felt. I wasn't completely honest. I said a 6, when I actually felt more like a 7 or an 8.

The yogurt drink helped calm me for a while. At least I had something in my hands to think about, something that offered comfort. But it didn't last long. My stomach was worse than I had imagined, and it was only getting worse.

We walked through a really nice shopping area. Ordinarily I would have been all over the place, shopping, trying on this and that, but looking around was all I could do, and I tried avoiding looking at food stalls. At a few points I felt like vomiting, but I suppressed the urge and distracted myself.

Steve said that their plan was to take me back to their house until I felt well enough to go to the night market. I'd been looking forward to seeing that night market for a while. I said that his plan sounded good, but in my head I honestly knew I should be taken back to the convent where the sisters were so I could lie down and rest. If I got sicker, and if I ended up really puking, I didn't want it to be with people I'd just met.

I plucked up the courage to tell them that, and Steve felt guilty for my illness. It wasn't his fault of course. It's no one's fault, but people tend to feel guilty for things anyway, and causing him to feel that guilt was what I feared most. It's bad enough that I felt sick. It's worse if I cause people around me to feel guilty.

When he took me back and on the bike I felt some waves of nausea, but I didn't have the urge to throw up, thankfully.

I came back to my room a little before five p.m. and collapsed in bed, then called out with the strength I had left, asking if anyone was home. Sr. Bertha came quickly, looked in and said, "Wow, you look like you're about to fall in love with your bed."

It's something you rub on your skin for curing a headache, a stomachache, a bug bite, or even a toothache. It literally is green oil, and it smells like incense.

I told her what had happened, and she offered me hot tea. At first I rejected it, but if it had a slight chance of helping, I thought I might as well try.

After taking a sip or two of the hot green tea, I took a nap. It was difficult, because it was hard to find a position which did not make me feel like I was about to vomit. In the end though, I never really threw up, though at one time I really wanted to, but couldn't.

Sr. Bertha came into my room to tell me to lift up my shirt so she could rub her magical green oil onto my tummy. Green oil is one of the widely used Taiwanese medicines, one that is supposed to help almost anything. It's something you rub on your skin for curing a headache, a stomachache, a bug bite, or even a toothache. It literally is green oil, and it smells like incense. It even works for zits, as I found out later. The only place you cannot put green oil is around the eyes because it will burn so much you will probably go blind. Green oil is popular because, for most people, it is curative and it feels soothing. It's something like that salve you rub on your chest at night when you have a bad cough. Green oil feels minty and stings your skin in a good way.

Sr. Bertha spread it on my stomach where it hurt. It didn't really help the pain I must admit, but it felt good in a burning kind of way. She also rubbed in some on my forehead. I felt very loved, and cared for. I was in bed, not moving, with my eyes closed, and there was Sr. Bertha, rubbing green oil on the places which hurt, and I didn't even ask her to. My heart swelled with thankfulness for her kindness.

My stomachache lasted the whole night. I watched a comedy movie on my iTouch to feel better. It helped my mood, but not my stomach. I ended up falling asleep to the sound of my music and woke up in the morning around seven.

I decided I would go to the English Mass today in another church. English Masses there were at 2:30, so I had a slow-paced morning. I began to plan out what to take to Taitung when I go there next Tuesday. I also watched a documentary on the Great Wall of China. I learned many things, but as usual, I do not remember most of it.

What did stick though is that the Great Wall of China, as it is known now, is not the true great wall, that it's only part of the true ancient wall which sretches for thousands of miles and is made with

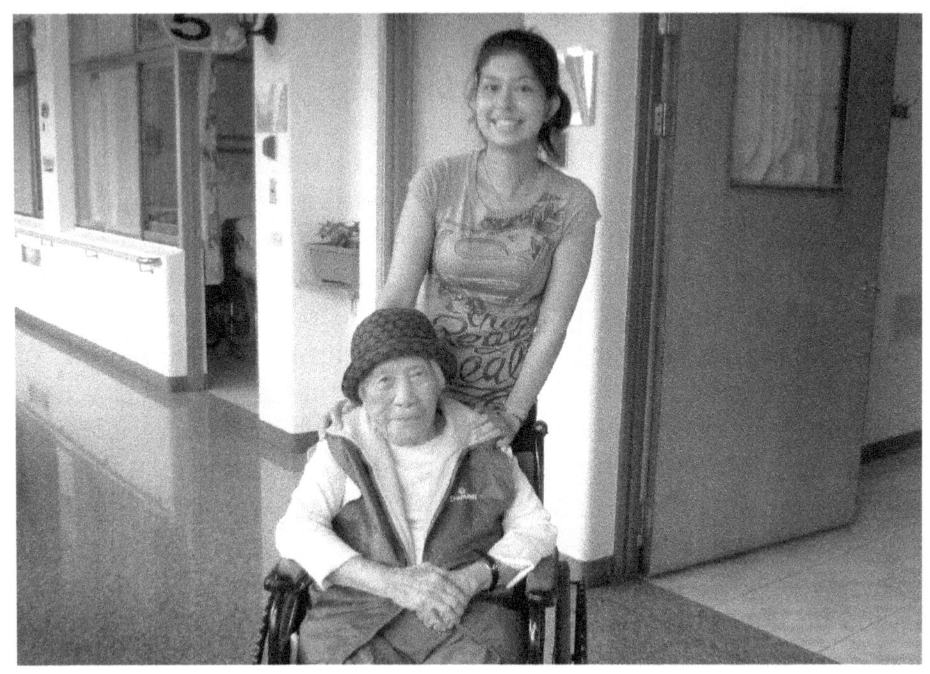

This resident of the care facility in Tainan worked for many years as a midwife.

the blood and bones of the peasants whose lives were sacrificed for the sake of the people. In some places of the ancient wall, the mortar is white because of crushed human bones. The wall, of course, was to keep the Huns and barbarians out. If all the walls built in different ages were connected, the resulting wall would circle the world twice and more. The Great Wall of China is also the longest, greatest graveyard in the world. Men spent their lives working on it, living apart from the comforts of their homes, most of them never to see the faces of their wives again. There is an ancient tale of the Wall of China that is apparently as famous as is the tale of Snow White in the US.

One of the wives of the workers decided to set out to meet her husband. Her husband, like many other men from her town had to work under the most horrid conditions in deserts and cold, dry lands. She brought clothes for him and some things which would be a reminder of home. She went to the closest watch tower and asked for her husband's whereabouts. The peasants and soldiers there knew the man and also knew of his recent death while building the wall.

Unable to tell her what had really happened they told her that he was not there, and to move onto the next watch tower. And so she walked to the next tower. The peasants and soldiers there also told her the same story because they did not have the heart to tell this passionate wife that her loved husband was already dead. So she was sent from one tower to the next, and she walked thousands of miles, from the beginning of the wall to the end of it near the ocean. At every stop, she hoped she would be reunited with her loved one. Finally, at the last fort, a man told her the truth about her husband. When she heard this news, she let out such a cry of anguish that part of the Great Wall collapsed.

When she heard this news, she let out such a cry of anguish that part of the Great Wall collapsed.

Today, tourists still visit that part of the wall where it had fallen and never again rebuilt. There is a temple dedicated to the woman, and the temple has a telescope for seeing the part of the wall that collapsed from the woman's cry of pain.

I have a hard time understanding a world in which such a story is as well known as the tale of Snow White. The Great Wall story tells of pain and hard work intertwining with everyday life and the constant fear of losing loved ones. Such a world strikes me as immeasurably sad and overwhelming.

Sr. Stella offered to walk with me to church for the English Mass. It took about thirty minutes. We talked a bit together, but it wasn't much. There was more silence than speech. It was an awkward silence, but what could I do about it? There was nothing in our conversation that changed what I had previously learned about her. Unfortunately, she told me no more heartwarming stories about her experiences with the AIDS patients. It was as if she knew that I found out she had worked in the office instead of with the actual patients. She still scares me, she still is so strict in everything. Her questions sound like demands, and I can only go along with what she asks.

Though the room was gloomy, I could sense his happiness and excitement for this venture we call marriage.

Before Mass began, I waited in Sr. Bertha's church office. She met with a young Filipino man who was preparing to get married. She helped him organize all the necessary papers. He looked excited, and though the room was gloomy, I could sense his happiness and excitement for this venture we call marriage. He was twenty-eight and had been dating his fianceé for the past five years. Sr. Bertha commented on how young he was, but he and I agreed that it was about the right age to get married. And after five years of waiting! But surprise over such a wait comes from Western culture. There in Taiwan or China, it's normal for women to get married in their mid-thirties. Of course, that limited the number of children she could have, and such birth control no doubt was sort of the reason for the wait.

Only Filipinos attended the English Mass. I had expected a more diverse group like the one in my parish church back in Japan, but I was wrong. The priest and I were the only non-Filipinos present.

The priest, an Indian, round with a bald head and big square glasses, looked as if he could be a professor. He never really opened his eyes during the Mass. Even during the sermon, it looked like he was closing his eyes. His Indian accent made me smile. I am by no means insulting his speech or making fun of it. It's just whenever I hear such an accent, it makes me happy. I love being around people with different accents.

The moment they sang the entrance song, my heart yearned to be back in my own church with my friends and family about me. The songs were exactly the same as the ones we sing in my parish church. It felt like someone was teasing me with candy I love through a HD television. I could just see myself in my church, and I could imagine my friends there, but no. I'm here, in Taiwan, in another church in the shape of a crucifix. Many people gave me those oh-so-conspicuous side glances because I was obviously a new face, and it was debatable if I was Filipino. One thing I can say, Filipinos aren't good at staring with discretion. I can't always tell when most people check somebody out or look at another person, but when Filipinos try for a clandestine stare, I can usually tell.

Anyway, I'm glad I didn't go to this English Mass earlier in my stay in Taiwan. Before I would have probably had another episode of culture shock, of feeling lonely. As I walked back to my temporary home, I thought about how much I missed my family and friends. I saw myself as a foreigner in Taiwan.

Then again, I am a foreigner wherever I go. I am lucky enough to be able to call Japan my home, but is it really my home? When I came back from the Philippines last December, for the first time in my life I didn't feel complete, I didn't feel at home in my own room and house. I felt like I left a part of myself in the Philippines. Of course, it may have been just me missing the family I had been staying with, but the feeling was something new and different for me. Surely feeling incomplete in your own home is one of the worst things you can feel.

I had a dream recently that dealt with my fear of change. It was a dream in which I came back from Taiwan to find that my parents had sold our house and moved into a tiny place, one packed with household goods from our bigger house. The new house was messy and disorganized like so many Taiwanese houses. In the dream we lived with another family, the very one I stayed with in the Philippines. There were three floors in the house in the dream; the first floor was the largest, and it could have been a great living room, but everyone had stored their extra furniture in the room, so there was hardly enough space to walk. The second floor was the bedrooms. There were several beds with no walls to separate the beds. On the third floor was a small kitchen and living room. It was dirty, messy, and tiny. I wanted to go home, but this was my home now. I had my family and friends around me, but I wasn't home.

Will this be my fate? Wandering between worlds, trying to find a place I can call my true home? Often, I am not a strong woman, but what weakens me the most is feeling isolated without a homey house and my family, for they are such a great part of my reason for being. I know I will see them in a few weeks, but maybe the home I once had will not be the same again. But, of course, it isn't just home that changes so that I can never truly find it again; everything changes though I might try to stop it, to stop what is inevitable with the movement of time. Everything changes. I change.

02/22

I haven't seen Elaine smile in ages. She has been so busy with paperwork that I hardly see her. Today she went to visit her ninety-one-year-old father, but as soon as she returned, she was at work in the office. She sits beside me in the morning at breakfast, but we haven't spoken more than a few words in days. When we do speak, it's usually because I ask a question about Chinese, and she immediately directs me to Sr. Stella or Sr. Francesca for an answer. I feel like our laughter and inside jokes have all drowned inside her, for she seems focused entirely on her stressful work. We are strangers living together, sitting together, and eating together. Even during the peace signs of the Mass, she doesn't smile at me. It's funny that small changes make such a strong impression on me. I thought I had a solid friendship with Sr. Elaine. Now she is a stranger.

I have been getting closer to Sr. Annie, though, because she often takes me out to show me around town. I have a virtual map in my mind now, better than the map in Sr. Stella's head or even Sr. Francesca's because they do not go out much. I think I'm better at road names than Sr. Annie herself because I remember the characters quicker since I am so familiar with them.

For lunch Sr. Annie took me to one of the oldest café restaurants she knows. The entrance is inconspicuous. Those not careful and mindful of finding the place will never find it. It just looks like a small gap between buildings. Since most structures are so crammed together, it isn't odd to see occasional gaps leading to alleyways between the stores. This appears to be one of them, but this alley leads to a narrow stairway, which leads up to a cozy and wonderful restaurant. No large person could fit into the entrance. If I stand at the entrance both my shoulders will be touching the sides of the walls, so I have to enter the place at a slant. I ordered Thai Lemon Fish. It was spicy and sour from being soaked in vinegar.

She told me about Sr. Paula's childhood, too, and how her father stored food in bomb shelters during World War II because there were constant air raids from Americans.

On the way to the restaurant, which takes about thirty minutes, I listened to more historically enriching stories of Sr. Annie's childhood. It's amazing how much she has experienced. She's only seventy-six, but the descriptions of her childhood are quite vivid. She has lived through World War II and the Korean War. She knows the names and even the sounds of the war planes because she lived near the military base where her father was stationed. She said that their family could hear the bombers flying over their house.

Her father trained the children to distinguish among types of airplanes through the sounds they make. She told me they heard many warplanes fly out. Her mother once woke the five children to say a prayer because they all knew something was up from the heavy sounds of planes. The next day war with Korean was declared. Those airplanes they heard the night before carried soldiers being sent to

Korea, many of whom never returned.

She told me about Sr. Paula's childhood, too, and how her father stored food in bomb shelters during World War II because there were constant air raids from Americans. One time, when Paula's family evacuated into a nearby cathedral, her first mother passed away. Sr. Annie wasn't sure why, but her mother died in that cathedral. Paula's father remarried, but Paula and her brothers and sister never accepted the new mother who was fourteen years old, and only a year or two older than the oldest daughter in their family. Before Paula left for the Philippines, she told me about the beatings the new young wife got because she did not do the housework as a woman should. "She was still fourteen," Sr. Paula said, "and she played with us instead of cooking dinner." Paula told me that her father beat her many times with a belt, and she often thought he had no reason for doing so.

During the war Paula's father was almost shot point blank.

During the war Paula's father was almost shot point blank. Japanese soldiers lined up a number of men to be executed for various crimes against the state, but one of the Filipino spies begged the Japanese to spare his professor, who was Paula's father. He had taught in a seminary. Since the Filipino spy gave up enough information and was going to be killed anyway, the Japanese soldiers agreed to spare him. Paula's father, from then on, helped to feed the Japanese soldiers as well as his family, which had increased to fourteen children since the new young wife bore many babies.

What a life I thought, and I wanted to know more about the kind of person her father was. I miss Paula, her dependence on my assistance, and her forgetfulness. She said she would write me when she gets to the Philippines, but I think she forgot about that too.

I went to see Magdalene after the rosary. When she heard the door open she turned around, saw it was me, and beamed. She waved her hands for me to come sit in front of her wheelchair. She told me she'd thought about me this whole weekend since I don't visit on Saturdays and Sundays. I asked in Chinese if she missed me, and she said yes. Her warmth makes my time with her one hundred

A care facility resident enjoying being outside

times more valuable.

Today she told me about her son who, while drunk, gave away over a thousand dollars to a temple by writing a check. I'm not sure exactly how it all came about because she was mainly speaking in Chinese, but I did understand that when she heard what he had done, she was shocked. I would be, too, I told her, for that was a large amount of money to give away. Magdalene felt so frustrated because she could not help her son now that he had almost no money.

"You are a good person." She said. "You bring happiness to everyone who meets you."

She changed the subject to religion and how being old is hard, but having her Buddhist belief and prayers has helped her everyday. She has a purpose, an end she is happy with. She pointed at the other old people on her floor and said, "They are the ones who are truly in pain. I have my God, my faith, and prayers. They have none." She told me Catholicism was a very good thing, too. "You are a good person." She said. "You bring happiness to everyone who meets you."

I will treasure those words forever.

She then pointed out that usually the people who come out of the chapel next to the convent are smiling after the service because they are carriers of joy and happiness. Magdalene sees this and respects Christianity because of it.

She talked about the future, too. She told me never to forget my experience in Taiwan. I told her never to forget me. She laughed, and she promised.

I told her that I am leaving tomorrow for a week, and she said to have fun while I am young. I think I will buy her some key chain or something from Taitung before I leave here permanently. I will miss our daily conversations, and I know she will too. I'm probably one of the only constant visitors she has. And, sad to say, I visit more often than her daughter does.

Tonight, I helped another lady with her meal. I felt a bit bad, because the woman I usually help kept staring at me while she was being assisted to eat by another caregiver. The lady I worked with today was the very woman who constantly mumbled and touched her face, but she was silent today all throughout her meal. She has her own teeth, still, so she chewed very well, and I helped her without making much of a mess. I think I'm pretty good at this because I've gotten the hang of putting the spoon into the mouth with the right amount of food so there won't be much spill. Some of the nurses, I notice, make a lot of mess. When I handled the soup, the other nurse was impressed with how cleanly I worked.

Score one for caring about how the woman feels as she is being helped to eat. Who would want to be messy? Even when I'm old, I think I will still want some form of manners.

I am also amazed at how much some older people can see. There's a cute and small elderly lady I see every morning at Mass and when I help people with meals. She always wears a knit hat and has a gleaming silver tooth. Her smiles and eyes remind me of my own grandmother. I think the lady with the silver tooth has a world-class smile. She sees me from far away and recognizes me, and she smiles every time I meet her eye. She doesn't wear glasses, and she can still eat by herself. I should find out how old she is next week when I come back from Taitung. I am leaving at eight tomorrow, catching the bullet train at 8:27.

The original plan for the trip to Taitung was for me to go with Sr. Francesca. Today, though, there was a change in plan. Since Sr. Francesca is so busy with her own preparations, Sr. Annie (Yes!) was to take me. It turned out marvelously. I knew I wasn't going to have much fun with Sr. Francesca. She's one of those people I just can't have a strong connection with, though I see her everyday and travel with her more than with the others. Now that I'm going with Sr. Annie, the trip will be different. I am looking forward to it, though it will mean a week without access to the internet.

02/23

The train going to Taitung (eastern Taiwan) was thirty-five minutes late. The ride takes about three hours. We left the convent home around eight in the morning. I said my goodbyes to Sr. Bertha, giving her a big, long hug. I saw that Magdalene was watching from the window like I told her to yesterday, so I waved goodbye to her.

When I first caught a glimpse of the mountains, I thought they were clouds.

Sr. Elaine's goodbye was abrupt and unemotional. She didn't even look up when she said goodbye. She held a bundle of her own laundry in her arms, and her body language told me she was quite preoccupied. Sr. Francesca was happy not to go, so her goodbyes were pretty cheerful. Apparently, the sisters' lifestyles are stricter where I am going; so of course I wondered what they will place on me. I would have been worried about feeling helpless, but I had Sr. Annie with me. She is herself part of my job because I take care of her, and I am her companion most of the time. I know she loves to talk, and it's hard for her in Taiwan when she cannot speak much English without being interrupted in Chinese. And despite her long years in Taiwan, she has not gotten the hang of the language. "Age fifty is not a good time to start learning a language," she often says. If I cannot please anyone there, I know I can still have a good time with Sr. Annie around.

Taitung's weather is almost tropical because the area faces a warm current in the Pacific Ocean. Through the windows on the right side of the train I could see the ocean right next to the tracks. From the windows on the left I could see the mountains.

When I first caught a glimpse of the mountains, I thought they were clouds. They were far away and high and since the air was so foggy and moist, I could only see faint outlines. I fell asleep and when I woke up, I could see both mountain and sea. The mountains looked dead in most parts because the trees had shed their leaves for the winter, and there were many large rocky areas where the typhoon Molokai had washed part of the mountain away. In some areas I could see the remnants of destroyed villages.

Another reason for the mountains looking so gray and dead was the terrible drought the southern and northern areas have been experiencing in the past year. No rain came during the rainy season. In Tainan city I couldn't really see the effects of the drought, but here it was obvious. The colors of the mountains faded from spots of green to brown, and the rivers had dried so they resembled dirt roads in a desert. The broken trees from the typhoon looked white and some stood like colossal ancient bones.

Sr. Gail, the sister servant from the community in Taitung, picked us up at the train station. Today I met the sisters who introduced me to their hospital. It was a smaller facility than the home for the elderly in Tainan, and it was clean and organized inside. The first floor was dedicated to the different areas of medical research and pediatricians. The second floor was under construction to become a new daycare system for the old people. The third floor was the hospice for the dying, who were mostly people afflicted with cancer. One of them had died the night before we arrived. They have the capacity to hold seven or eight cancer patients, but when I arrived, there were six.

When I found out that Mass was at 6:30, I took a quick shower and got to bed early so I wouldn't be too sleepy in the morning.

02/24

I was many things today: a cook, an assistant for the elderly, a shopper, a gardener, a social worker, and finally, now at my keyboard, a writer.

The day started out vague. I knew I was going to experience new things, but I wasn't sure if I was up for any of them. The memory of how I felt at first in Tainan haunted me. Will the next few days make this trip worthwhile?

She smiles, but I can tell it's not something her face was meant to do much of the time.

The sisters I have met have been pleasant. I met Sr. Jane, and she and Sr. Annie and I had stimulating conversations in our free time. Sr. Jane left today, and I'm going to miss her subtle Louisiana accent.

Sr. Gail is Vietnamese. I have few things to say about her because I don't know her. However, she seems to be a strict and serious person. She smiles, but I can tell it's not something her face was meant to do much of the time. The way she interacts, the way she talks, and the way she acts, pretty much the way she is, suggests that she is the head of the community. In the communities of the Daughters of Charity, one is not supposed to know the head by the way she acts, but I guess here is an exception. Also, this may be a mistake on my part, but I sense an aura of slight haughtiness in her. I really can't be sure where this originates, or even if she is haughty or not. I just got that feeling soon after I met her. I'd like to find out, but she's one of those sisters who is almost impossible to get close to and, simply put, I don't feel like making that effort. She is a busy woman and too serious for me.

The place I'm staying in is right next to the hospital. This hospital has been in Taitung for such a long time that many of the patients were born here and returned as adults for healthcare. It used to be a hospital for many diseases, but now the upper floors are mainly a hospice for cancer patients. As I said before, there are currently six people on the third floor who are dying of cancer.

Since the first floor is mainly a pediatric center, I saw many babies and parents waiting to get vaccines. The babies were all darling, but unlike some girls, I'm happy just looking at them once in a while. Babies have such startling mood swings. Even a child can switch from ultra happy to super unhappy in less than one minute.

The sisters' house is shaped like a huge rectangle with an impressive yard in the middle that holds a pond. There are some fish in the pond, and frogs. One sister told me that you can hear the frogs at night, though I think frogs are now hibernating through winter. I say "winter," but in reality it is more like early summer weather to me. I got a tan today just walking outside with Sr. Annie.

The room where I stay has to be the oldest in the house. There's one very small sink, a hospital bed-chair, and an old desk with a broken study lamp. There's also a big wardrobe, but it's worn out and drab beyond any hope of magic, much less opening to some vision of *Narnia*. I wish it did open to some place magical, for it would be a nice escape from this gloomy room.

The bed is a bit softer than the one back in Tainan. There's no bathroom in my room, so I have to go out and walk to my right to get to the bathroom. The bathroom contains a shower that's larger and cleaner than other showers I've encountered in Taiwan. There are many mosquitoes though. Everywhere I turn I see two or three.

I think I've figured out why I can't feel at home in a Taiwanese residence. It has to do with two main things: one is the floor, and the other are the lights. In most homes and rooms, the floors are made from stone or marble. It's not a pretty kind of stone. The typical Taiwanese floor consists of ugly gray rock, sometimes with white pebbles. These floors remind me of my old school corridors. In Japan and America I became accustomed to seeing a lot of wood on the floor, or even carpet. In Taiwan it's constantly gray and gloomy, and I always have the feeling I have to be doing something or else the room will eat me with boredom. The artificial lights also play a big part. The lights in my room are white, the fluorescent kind that often hum. I honestly hate that kind of light. I mean, its okay in an office or in school because that's where they usually are anyway. But not in personal rooms. I have grown up with a soft yellow light which lit up the room like a large candle. The bathroom here is like that, and I think that's mainly the reason why I don't mind the dirtiness of the bathroom so much. My room in Tainan has a yellow study lamp that lights up the whole room too, so I enjoy staying in my room there, even though the floors are the ugly stone. I avoid my room here though, because it has both the white lights and the ugly floor.

Since someone broke into this house last year, the sisters have put locks on almost every door.

Caroline and the daughter of one of her teachers with a neighborhood boy who wanted to be in the picture

Since someone broke into this house last year, the sisters have put locks on almost every door. Thus, I have to carry around keys wherever I go. I have a key to the main door and a key to my own room. Having these keys makes me feel like a responsible person. I like the feeling of having to lock and unlock the door to my roomeach time I go in and out. Plus, the key to my room looks like an old key, like those ancient keys with a fork at the end. I always wanted to open things with that type of key, and now that desire has become reality. That's one thing I like about this place.

There are five sisters staying here, and including me and Sr. Annie there are seven now at the dinner table. Other people live here other than the sisters, like the nurses from the hospital, but I don't see them much.

I had to wake up earlier than I usually do today because Mass was at 6:30 instead of 7:00. I set my alarm at 6:10 and barely made it. The priest was bald with big square glasses. He was a pediatrician before he became a priest. His voice was unusually soft. People on the rear pews probably heard only mumbling during the Mass, and the chapel isn't even that big! His sermons are louder though, for some reason. He is an obvious introvert. Mass is probably an exception to his silent ways because he has to say certain things in a certain way.

Today at breakfast she taught me a new word in Taiwanese, one that means "empty head." We are going to get along fine.

During Mass today I realized I have memorized most of the responses in Chinese, though I'm not exactly sure what they mean. Back home in Tainan, I always read the *pin-yin*, or phonetic spelling, but since I forgot to bring it today, I had to rely on others and my memory. I did pretty well, I think, but I know I cannot say them by myself. I can say certain prayers without a problem when I'm with a group of people saying the same thing, but if I had to do it alone, I'd probably not be able to say a thing. Community is important that way.

At breakfast Sr. Diana asked if I had any dreams last night. Sr. Diana is a native here from one of the aboriginal tribes. She is a large lady and looks sort of Filipino. She has very dark skin on her face and thick black eyebrows with large eyes. The moment I met her, I knew she was the sister I'd probably become most attached to here. The way she laughs is so loud and so long. She continues laughing at something I thought was funny only for three seconds. So I end up laughing with her because her laugh is contagious and for the sake of laughing. Today at breakfast she taught me a new word in Taiwanese, one that means "empty head." We are going to get along fine.

I told her I had a dream about running water. It was more complicated than that. My dream was a story about breaking hearts, and hearts being broken. There was water and a man. I saw the dream in the third person as well as the first. In the beginning I was the water—literally I was water itself. Then I was the man who was supposed to marry this water who was alive and who spoke normally. In the end the man decided (or I decided) that I didn't want to get married, so I broke the water person's heart. It was an odd sensation, because I played both part and felt both pains. Sr. Diana, who didn't know all these details, told me that running water means that good luck is coming. Well sister, if you knew the whole story I doubt you'd say that. But then again, she's only looking at the generic symbol of running water. She is also from a superstitious tribe, so I hope what she tells me comes true. The natives from any country, may it be Taiwan, Australia, or North and South America, have many symbols and are usually very religious.

In the morning I was a cook. One of the ladies who lives in this apartment complex was making the delicious Chinese dumplings. Sr. Diana told her that I would be helping, and she was happy with that. Many Chinese people love to teach cooking, perhaps because to them it's like spreading their own culture. She didn't speak any English, and her Chinese was a bit hard to understand. She is from mainland China, and has been making these dumplings probably since she was my age or younger.

The way she kneaded the bread as well as made the thin wrappings of the dumpling was all with a set rhythm and very fast. When she made the thick sheets of wrapping, she did it so fast and it looked so easy. However, when I attempted, I failed at it the first time. I could not get any of the rhythm and failed to keep the wrapping round. Mine turned out more of a square or a retarded circle. I was very slow, too. Something that took her five seconds took me one minute. My first job was the easiest, though it was hard on my arms. I had to chop the cabbage into very small pieces. I had the classic rectangular large knife. It was heavy, so every time I chopped, it made a loud noise. I'm not sure how sharp it was, but I was chopping the cabbage mainly with the force of the knife hitting the cut board. I had a lot to chop, and my arms soon became tired. It was an inspiring job though and a good way to release stress. I personally didn't have any stress at all, but after I chopped the cabbage in fine pieces, I had a sense of accomplishment.

I tried writing down the ingredients and the way she cooked the dumplings so I can make them back at home. The instructions I wrote are vague, though, and I'll probably lose the paper I wrote everything on. Typical of me. One thing that struck me was that she put a lot of oil in the meat. And the oil just had to be soybean oil, so it condemned all my dumplings to hell because I won't be able to eat them, given my allergy to soy products and peanuts. In some ways it's horrible living here where everyone loves peanuts. Some eat them after every meal. And they love tofu so much that many will eat it rotten. It smells like dead flesh and old farm animals.

It surprised me a bit to be so willing to get muddy and sandy.

I took a walk with Sr. Annie after lunch. My lunch consisted of a potato because I wasn't feeling very good in the stomach after eating the dumplings. I had eaten three small ones, knowing the damage they could do to my stomach. I just couldn't resist. On the bright side is the possibility of losing some weight here, given all the foods I must avoid.

At two o'clock Sr. Diana took me to her workplace in the hospital. She is actually CEO. I didn't know that until she showed me her card. Anyway, my first job as her social worker was to tend to the new garden on the second floor. As I've said, the second floor is being renovated for the new home for the elderly. They have a large balcony there, and workers have been planting flowers and different kinds of grass so it will be nice and peaceful to look at. Thus, I was a gardener for about an hour. Since I've seen my mother garden a lot at home, I knew my way around. I actually designed where the flowers would go and did all the hard labor of moving dirt, watering, fertilizing, and planting. I got my hands plenty dirty, all the way up to my elbows. It surprised me a bit to be so willing to get muddy and sandy. I thought I would hate getting dirty, but it was fun, and it made me remember my childhood when I often played with plants, dirt, and bugs. Plus, good dirt—the kind flowers need—isn't that dirty. I ended up enjoying the gardening. I planted hydrangeas, some small moss, a rose bush, and other flowers I am not familiar with. Often I pray for understanding, and perhaps today one of those prayers was answered, for today, I understood why gardeners garden.

Last night I developed a swollen redness around my eye like something bit me or someone punched me. This morning it was worse, and I could see only half as much from that eye. My acne is worse, too. The air is nicer here, since there are more green plants to filter it, and nicer yards. Mountains with their clean air stand closeby. So I wonder why my skin is getting worse instead of better. There must be some reason, and hope I'll get something from staying here. And I have so far.

The first night here I started to count down the days until I go back to Tainan because I felt like I wouldn't like it here much, but my swollen eye actually got much kind attention from all the sisters and eventually from a doctor who declared that I have some kind of bacterial infection due to the climate change, and he gave me medicine. That's the part of my stay here when I was a patient. He told me that my acne wasn't really pimples and perhaps the medicine he prescribed will clear up the problems on my face.

The medicine is colorful. Apparently the Chinese love for bright colors runs deeper than I thought because the medicine was of multiple and exotic colors including bright yellow, green, pink, and orange. Treating the acne or whatever I had made my day more interesting and certainly more colorful.

The markets and streets of Taitung are pretty much similar to the ones in Tainan, but smaller and more compact. The street names don't always have *pin-yin* (a new phonetic spelling) underneath, probably because this place is less international (*pin-yin* is a kind of phonetic spelling using letters from a much older Chinese alphabet). I haven't seen any foreigners except the sisters I live with. There is one thing that makes Taitung and Tainan very different. There is something missing here that there is plenty of in Tainan. Can you guess? It's all the temples. The beautiful and gaudy temples are almost at every corner in Tainan, but here I haven't seen many. The reason is simple. Most people living here are either Catholic or Protestant. If I translate directly the Chinese into English, the Catholics are called "God's reli-gion" or "God's Church" and the Protestants are called "Jesus Church." Many people here openly greet the sisters with "Good morning, Sister" and not just a "Good morning." In Tainan you would never see that happen. There aren't many Buddhists here.

The mother said that bullying and the criticism from her neighbors for having three disabled children was too overwhelming for her.

I'd like to share one of the stories Sr. Annie told me while on our walk (where I was an assistant for the elderly, and a shopper by buying myself a beautiful purple skirt that could be a dress as well.)

In most cultures having children with special needs, especially those with mental handicaps, is looked down upon. Children's disabilities are blamed on the mother. The mother, of course, needs so much love in her heart to care for the special child. As Sr. Annie said, special children need special parents. There was a woman that Sr. Annie knew well who had three children with special needs. One day Sr. Annie found her crying in her kitchen. When asked why, the mother said that bullying and the criticism from her neighbors for having three disabled children was too overwhelming for her. She said her neighbors call her bad names and claim she is cursed.

Sr. Annie gave her another perspective. Having one special child is tough, but having three, she said, now that's something for a very special woman. Not many women have love enough to care for these children, and it takes a wonderful woman to care for three. Sr. Annie said to the woman, "Have you ever thought that God gave you these three for a reason? You have more love in your heart than most women in the world, so maybe these children are yours for a reason. It takes someone strong and special to bring up three special children. God never gives you more than He knows you can handle."

Then the woman stopped crying.

For some reason, this story brought tears to my eyes. I got chills just thinking about her and all the hardships in raising these three children. And how much love, oh the love, she has to have for these children. She is surely a great woman.

I'd like to write more about today, but I am very sleepy. The medicine I took for my skin might have made me drowsy. But mostly, I think it was the sun and all the walking with Sr. Annie and all the gardening that fatigued me. I will be going out with Sr. Diana again tomorrow, this time to a village where there are people who can speak Japanese. I hope for another eventful day.

02/25

My eye is less swollen today, but it is still red. Since I have bad blood circulation, I have dark patches under my eyes, so it looks as if I have a black eye. I would normally be self-conscious at home in Japan when I go out, but here I don't mind. I sometimes forget how I look, though when I catch a glimpse of myself in passing windows or mirrors I flinch. I've hoped to stop caring though, and now is a good time for me to stop worrying about looks. Appearance is so superficial anyway.

Sr. Annie tagged along with me and Sr. Diana. The drive to the village was one of the best ever. As I turned up the music playing "Unchained Melody" (one of my all-time favorites), I rolled down the window of the Volkswagon van and took in the sea breeze and the mountain air. The wonderful scenery included both high and magnificent mountains as well as the great Pacific Ocean at the same time. The mountains were jagged, high, and pointy. Most had clouds covering the tops like great giants wearing white veils. The sides of many mountains were eroded, rocky, exotic, and wild in a breath-taking way. Today, I came to understand why Taiwan is called

Two sisters dining on dumpings in a restaurant in Tainan

Formosa, or "Beautiful Country." I had been blinded by all the pollution and buildings of the city, but here the true nature of the island commanded my attention and awe. Orange trees, banana trees, and types of grapefruit grow in seeming wild profusion. There are coconut trees and betel nut trees.

I had never heard about the betel nut till I came to Taiwan. It is a locally grown nut which strikes me as a kind of recreational drug. Many elderly women chew betel nuts, and in Taipei they are sold by young women wearing scanty clothing. The nut contains bright red juice that people spit out on the streets. The red juice always looked like blood to me. The betel nut is supposed to give you a mild type of high. The government tried to ban them but met much resistence, and the nut is available abundantly. Perhaps chewing betel nuts is like drinking alcohol. Even some children partake. Perhaps it is like tobacco, too, in that it can cause cancer in the mouth. I once tried a nibble but couldn't stand the taste, which was something like the smell of certain pungent field weeds. So I gave the nut to Sr. Diana, who loves them. She bought a couple of bags of betel nuts when we went to the village.

Sr. Diana's tribe, the Ami tribe, chooses its leaders from women. Men are inferior to woman in this tribe.

The old people I got to talk to were mostly dark-skinned people from several different aboriginal tribes. There used to be seven main tribes in the Taitung area and in the mountains, but for years their numbers dwindled. However, since the government began to encourage the preservation of their aboriginal culture and heritage, the people of the tribes have grown in number.

Many of the old people we met could speak pretty good Japanese, so I didn't have a problem communicating with them. They were mostly women. I met three of Sr. Diana's older sisters. She is the youngest of six girls, and the oldest has died. One is in Taipei recovering from a stroke, and the rest live here in the mountains. All the woman are over sixty-five, and none of them had glasses on, or even had a wheelchair. Their good health probably has to do with the exercise they get walking in the mountains and their diet.

Sr. Diana's tribe, the Ami tribe, chooses its leaders from women. Men are inferior to woman in this tribe. If I understand right, the women get to keep their family name even at marriage. Sr. Diana is one of the leaders of her family, as she is the youngest and most responsible.

On the ride back to the city, Sr. Diana let us drop by a couple of tourist spots. One was a nice café with a beautiful view. I had a caramel macchiato for the first time, something I much enjoyed. It started to shower when we got out of the car. The clouds hung low, dark, and gray. I have said before that gray is a gloomy color, especially on the floor in a room, but I think there's nothing more beautiful than dark gray in the sky when clouds are pregnant with water and the green on the mountains turns a darker shade of green with plants anticipating a coming rain. The ocean gave out a beautiful shade of blue during the shower as well. The rain didn't last long, but the cloud stayed a while, so I was able to take a few beautiful pictures of the beach and mountains.

Another tourist spot is a place where a river runs uphill.

Another tourist spot is a place where a river runs uphill. The stream of water looks pretty ordinary until you see the leaves going uphill with the current. The water appeared to be running up the hill instead of down it. I have never seen such a stream. Many Chinese consider it a miracle, and many tourists visit here. The natives don't think it's a big deal, though. Personally, I don't know what to make of it. I witnessed water seeming to run against gravity.

I also took the classic "hug the coconut tree" picture. I always wanted to do that, and I did today. The photo didn't turn out as artistic as I thought it would, so I was a bit disappointed. I'll try again someday.

We got back around 2:30 p.m. We had left at quarter past eight, so we were out for a full six hours. I tried watching some TV but nothing interesting was on, so I ended up taking a walk around the neighborhood with Sr. Annie. I dropped by a lingerie shop for fun. The majority of underwear and bras were red, for red is supposed to be the luckiest of colors. During the Chinese New Year, you are supposed to buy new everything. Even underwear. People like to buy red underwear in order to have good luck during the coming year. Also, many believe that women will have more luck with men if the women wear red panties and red bras. The red lingerie I looked at had designs on each piece. Some of them had a tiger as this is the year of the tiger, and some had designs of money and gold. I didn't buy any, though. Nothing looked comfortable. It seemed all for show, and nothing for comfort. I am a picky shopper when comes to clothing. I want comfort and style, and a reasonable price. And I have patience enough to wait for the right moment to buy it.

Sr. Annie and other sisters end up calling me "sister" when they want my attention. Especially Sr. Annie. I have spent more time with her than any other sister by now. She calls me "sister" without even realizing it. Like today, I analyzed the personalities of Sr. Diana and Sr. Gail and guessed they had a hard time getting along. She was pretty impressed that I caught on so fast. "You would be a natural psychologist, sister," she said with a smile. I might as well be one of them, and I kind of want to wear a habit to see how it feels, and I've lived with them like I was part of their community. But I don't want to become a nun. I still want to get married some day. Sr. Annie encourages that too. At least she encourages girls to go to a university first, to have some work and life experience, and even fall in love before deciding to become a sister.

02/26

Yesterday I had the most annoying night ever. I battled with a mosquito. It may sound easy, but it's not. I never really hated mosquitoes until I got here. Taiwanese mosquitoes have a habit of buzzing around your ears while you sleep. Sr. Patrica called it their "manner" to let us know that they're coming to get some blood. It's not the low buzz of a fly or a stink bug, but it's very high. I pulled the covers over my ears and face and hoped it would go away. I had a dream about earthquakes, and later I learned that there had been a large earthquake in Japan and Chili.

This morning, I saw what had to be the same mosquito that annoyed me in the night. I smacked it, and I killed it. But I saw some of my blood stain the white wall. The mosquito was probably too full to react when I swatted it. Serves her right. I don't know where she bit me. I hope it's not on my face again.

Today I had another long drive along the beach and mountains to visit patients who were too far away to come to the sisters for help, or unable to come to the hospital except for every once in a while. We had seven patients on the list today. Sr. Lucinda took me and one of the young nurses. Sr. Lucinda is Vietnamese and so far the youngest Daughter of Charity I've met in Taiwan. She's forty-one years old. She has a delightful laugh and a big smile. You can hardly see her eyes when she smiles, and her teeth are straight and white. When she smiles you can see both the top and bottom teeth. She's very short, and she can speak some English, and we get along pretty well. She doesn't give out the serious aura that Sr. Gail does, nor is she a crazy joker like Sr. Diana. She's actually right in between. I like her balance.

On the beautiful drive to the villages, I decided that I was a true islander. It may sound odd because living in Japan my whole life you would think I already considered myself an islander. But the truth is I never really knew how much the mountains and sea moved my heart and soul until they were taken away from me and reintroduced again. I have spent the last month or more in the middle of a polluted city with no mountains. I went to the sea once, but something was missing. Where were the mountains? The city where I live in Japan has both. The drive to remote villages has that and more. The mountains, I think, were more beautiful than the ones in Japan, but such a conclusion may be just because I hadn't paid so much attention to the mountains before. Still, I swear these mountains are way higher than those of Japan, and more pointy and steep. If there ever was a Jurassic Park, it would have to be here.

The mountains are much closer to the ocean than in Osaka, my city in Japan. These high mountains seemed almost to arise out of the blue Pacific, an ocean that here has many shades, light blue where it is shallow and a clear line between the dark blue of deeper water and the light blue shades.

The day was a sunny one with no clouds to smoke the sky. It was one that made me want to jump into the water to cool myself. We made some stops to go to the bathroom since it was a long drive. Unexpectedly, the public bathrooms were among the cleanest I've experienced in Taiwan. They actually had rolls of toilet paper, and they had soap. I appreciated that there were European toilets instead of the squatties. These public toilets were cleaner than those of many homes I had visited in Taiwan. I wondered who keeps these public restrooms in order. In Japan or even in the U.S., such public restrooms can be the most disgusting places, but here it is the opposite. Anyway, at each bathroom stop there is also a resting place outside with a beautiful view of the ocean and mountains. I wanted to drive on this road forever, but alas, we had work to do.

I wanted to drive on this road forever, but alas, we had work to do.

I found out that these home visits we were making were mainly to help those who are bedridden and need to have their urine tubes changed, or breathing tubes changed, or their bedsores cleaned.

The first man we visited was a cheerful person. He was no doubt once good looking sometime in the past. He wasn't terribly old either, and his peculiar looks were the result of being paralyzed from the chest down. He could move his head and arms, but nothing else. His mother took care of him. Their house was cleaner than most, and we had to take our shoes off at the door, which was a first for me in Taiwan.

Most bedridden people we visited were between thirty and sixty years old, and most had been paralyzed at a young age due to a motorcycle accident. The first man we visited had been in such an accident, too. Since he had been bedridden for the longest time, probably years by the looks of him, his legs were almost as thin as my wrists. He was a high-spirited man, though. A wheelchair by his bed was evidence that he could at least move around some beyond the bedroom. I wasn't allowed in the room while the nurse changed his tube, and I waited with Sr. Maria.

Sr. Maria has a degree and license in nursing, but since she got her education in Vietnam, her license is meaningless here. Even though she knows exactly what to do, technically she is not supposed to do work that requires a licensed nurse. She helps the nurse in procedures, but she does not do the work by herself. She said it's too difficult to get a license in Taiwan because of the language and because she is a foreigner. Taiwan has been active in trying to get the locals to do the jobs that the Filipino migrants and Vietnamese migrants are doing. Just a few years ago, thousands of Filipino migrants were sent back to the Philippines. It's great that the country is encouraging the locals to do different jobs to increase the wealth of the economy, but the problem is many Taiwanese do not want to do the work the migrants are doing because they consider it dirty work: taking care of the old, the sick, and the poor. But I'm writing in broad generalizations, which are usually partly false as well as partly true.

While I had seen similar procedures on television, it was a first to see such a process in real life.

The second person we visited needed only her feeding tube changed. She was probably in her seventies. She had white hair and could still walk with her cane. The feeding tube was in her throat. I didn't know you could have something so large and so heavy in your throat for so long. The nurses came to change it monthly for sanitary reasons, I presumed. The tube was metal. I didn't get to touch it or feel it, but it looked pretty heavy and looked to be one centimeter or more in diameter. While I had seen similar procedures on television, it was a first to see such a process in real life. The hole was large, about the diameter of my finger. It wasn't bleeding or anything. I guess it's like body piercing; after a while, the hole becomes part of the skin. It was not red or raw looking because she'd had this tube for such a long time. It looked painful to see that thick curved metallic tube go down her throat ten centimeters or so. The procedure took a while to prepare because the nurse had to make sure everything was completely sterilized. I watched the procedure a few times, so I could probably tell exactly how to do it, if I had the kit with me.

One of the residents Caroline visited daily

When the new tube was inserted and the lady coughed through the tube, it looked painful. It probably felt like something forcefully entering your throat, so your natural impulse is to cough to get it out. After a few coughs she was okay, though. Because of the tube she cannot make much sound when she tries to speak. She tried to say something, but all I heard was some disturbing noise. To get any words out she had to put her hand over the metal tube so the air would not escape from there. When we left she stopped up the hole in her throat and said, "thank you."

I eavesdropped on the Chinese conversation happening on the other side of the curtain.

The nurse dropped by a couple of houses to give people medicine for the month. Sr. Maria and I stayed in the car while she made the deliveries. In other houses I found two patients whose conditions so disturbed me that I decided I'm not fit to be a nurse.

One of the patients was a woman in her early thirties. She had a motorcycle accident when she was twenty-four if I understood right, and had been paralyzed from the chest down since then. If she opened the doors to her room, she would see the magnificent beauty of the mountains right at her doorstep. She was in a green medical bed when we entered. She had been turned away from us as we came in, and she didn't seem to react to our presence. For a moment I thought she was in a coma, but then she turned toward us, but she didn't look at us. At a glance I could see pain and regret in her face.

Her mother had been taking care of her for the past few years. The mother looked too old to have such a young daughter. Soon I found out that the paralyzed daughter was the youngest of eight children. The mother, who was in her seventies, spoke with me in Japanese.

I noticed many of the older people claim they could not speak Japanese, but as I urged them to speak, they understood almost everything and responded in Japanese.

Sr. Maria and the nurse got to work with the paralyzed woman doing the usual checking of temperature and blood pressure. There was a curtain around the bed, so I did not see any of it. While they were working I talked to the mom.

I eavesdropped on the Chinese conversation happening on the other side of the curtain. They were talking about me, something that got my attention. The woman was asking who I was, and the nurse was telling her. Though my Chinese is still not so good, I understood what they were saying about me.

When the procedure was finished, the paralyzed girl looked a bit more lively. I heard her talk more, and when the nurse drew the curtain, the girl put on her glasses so she could see. She was a beautiful woman, and she looked younger than she was. Her hair was long and black with a lovely sheen that I envied. Her arms were a bit chubby, as was her face, but that didn't change the fact she was a good-looking woman. Her arms were probably the only place where she had some muscle since her lower body was paralyzed. I wondered how many days she cried herself to sleep, how many months went by with nothing extraordinary in her life after her social life and physical activities were taken away so abruptly and so tragically in the prime of her youth.

Her suffering has made her highly attuned to the feelings of others.

People who think motorcycles are just a convenience and safe should visit these bedridden people, feed them, bathe them, and change their diapers. Surely the most die-hard motorcycle enthusiasts would change their minds. After seeing her so weak and wretched I would understand if she fell into a suicidal depression. Every visitor, every person who lays eyes on her would surely feel pity for her, but I doubt anyone's response could match the despair felt by the woman herself.

Without doubt she knows we feel sorry for her. Her suffering has made her highly attuned to the feelings of others. I wondered if with every glance at us she might feel strong pangs of jealousy and envy, for we can walk, talk, move, and do simple things that are so difficult for her like going to the bathroom. Even worse would be all the regret for her injuries, regret which will haunt her until she dies. I wondered if each time she sees a visitor, her natural instinct is to know the other's feelings as they look at her, and if seeing such pity and horror in others is a reminder of her own condition. How many more years does she have until she dies? Who will take care of her after her mother dies? The days must pass slower for her than they do for me, and anger with herself and maybe even with those who come to see her must be overwhelming at times.

The second woman I saw was in worse condition, but she was also older. I am uncertain how she came to be so afflicted, though it was clear she has been that way for several years. The certificate for her family members to take care of her medically looked pretty old and worn out. She had a feeding tube, a catheter, a horrid bedsore, and a tube in her nose. She could not speak or move her body. Her eyes twitched constantly and her hand trembled. The son, or brother, of this woman took care of her daily by changing diapers and feeding her through a metallic tube. A nurse came every month to change the tubes and sanitize the sores. During this procedure, I was allowed to observe everything.

I've never seen something look so painful and so incurable.'

The tube changing for the throat took a bit more effort and caused more pain than it did for the first woman I saw. This lady coughed a couple more times, and I saw tears sliding down her face, though she could not say a word. The nurse did not change the catheter; she said it wasn't time yet. But she did take a look at a bed-sore right below the lowest back bone. It wasn't bloody, though it was red and angry-looking and was the size of my pinky in diameter. I've never seen something look so painful and so incurable. The nurse pressed around it a couple of times and used a lot of gauze to cover the sore so it wouldn't start bleeding or get infected.

The changing of the tube in the woman's nose was painful to watch. I didn't know that tube went so deep down. It went all the way to the bottom of the lungs. The tube was thick, like 0.8 centimeters. When the nurse started to pull the tube out, I thought it would never end. I watched the procedure in stunned silence wondering all the while if I should leave or at least turn and look away. After the nurse put in a new tube, she put water in it. I do not know where the water went or exactly why the nurse used it, but I kept watching and feeling surprised that I could witness such difficult and intimate healthcare.

During this session I saw the elderly woman completely naked, saw her open sore, and saw those frightful tubes go everywhere into her body. I was not disgusted nor turned off. There is nothing repulsive about the human body. But I did realize that, given my natural impulse to feel empathy and to sympathize, it would be a bad idea for me to pursue a career as a nurse, for I could easily become depressed, perhaps to the point of being despondent. I wanted to bless the woman, cry over her, touch her, anything I could do to help make her better. And the mere thought of being unable to ease her suffering caused me to squirm in anguish as my heart moved toward the woman. I knew in that moment that I could not take such experiences every day. It would be so hard to do the job of this efficient and competent nurse who daily sees such suffering.

I have not seen too much in my life. On the contrary, I have seen too little. I live in a bubble, in my own reality. Seldom do I realize how ephemeral and fragile my comfortable reality is. In moments like the one in that room with the busy nurse and the suffering woman, my reality seems close to a lie. How happily I can live everyday with joy, complaining about troubles that are not really troubles at all. In my comfortable life I know nothing of these bedridden people's reality and their lives of constant staring into nothingness.

Would I want to die if I were one of them? Some may say that it is not good to compare our lives with those of suffering people because doing so will only make us feel bad. But sometimes it is a good thing to compare ourselves with those who are unfortunate to remind us of how blessed we are to have the ability to wake up in the morning, sit up, and walk into the bathroom to wash our faces, to choose what to see and do that day and the next. We still have dreams, we still have desires that are yet to become reality. What do they have, these maimed and suffering people? And yet in this fragile life so prone to accident and illness, these things so normal to us might be taken away in a second—as they were in the moment of the paralyzed girl's motorcycle accident. The true humiliation, the misery, and the vexation of those who are paralyzed cannot be felt and fully understood by the rest of us who live in our various comfortable bubbles. We should strive for understanding. I should strive.

I wish we could all share our health and youth. The world is unbalanced, yet it keeps spinning. We are unbalanced, ignorant of most realities and often we live without thinking, without thankfulness for good limbs, eyesight, movement, and the ability to taste and communicate, yet our lives keep spinning. Perhaps we find balance only when we lose it. Behind the earth's beauty Mother Nature bears all pain, all suffering, not merely beauty and joy, though the positives are there, too.

I had to stay in the car for the last patient because he had scabies. During the time I was alone, I wrote these thoughts in a notebook.

On the way back from a full day of visits and driving, the ocean with its perpetual waves did not look as beautiful as it did before.

My day wasn't finished though, because I got a shot today. The red lumps and itchy areas increased on my face and even on my hands. It looked pretty bad. I had three spots under my eye, and now one on top of my left eye, making me look puffy and swollen again. Sr. Diana took me back to the doctor at night, and the doctor decided to give me different kinds of medicine as well as a shot to help the allergic reaction I was having to something. I saw the nurse load the hypodermic needle with a clear liquid, then inject it into me. My arm felt numb after that, and I felt better as Diana and I joked around in the car.

All I could think was that her purchase looked just like drug deals I had seen on TV. But, of course, it was not like that in reality.

She didn't go directly home but instead bought two more bags of betel nuts. Sr. Diana didn't even get out of the car to buy them. She slowed down in front of a dirty store with one man sitting in the front, watching TV. When he saw her, he went to a refrigerator for the two bags she wanted. The transaction happened within a minute or so and through the window of the car. All I could think was that her purchase looked just like drug deals I had seen on TV. But, of course, it was not like that in reality.

Some of the sisters probably think Sr. Diana has a bad habit. Well, it's not a good habit since many things added in processing the betel nut cause cancer of the mouth. I think chewing betel nuts is not like taking narcotics. The strong drugs are too dangerous to even experiment with because they grab you so you can't let go. Seeking whatever small high betel nuts offer and even wanting the caffeine rush available in chocolates and coffee are drug behaviors of a sort. So, I believe we shouldn't judge or be critical of a person for buying betel nuts. It's when drug behavior focused on bad drugs so they become the central pull of your everyday existence that you need to worry. Then buying and taking drugs becomes sinful, evil, and destructive. Sr. Diana's minor addiction—if it is a real addiction —to these nuts is something I hope she could easily stop. So with a lovable woman like her and with her fixation similar to that of a chocoholic I can't help smiling and remaining silent as she pauses to buys another packet or two of betel nuts. Many people ingest minor drugs, and moderation is necessary. I know she has it, so why worry, right?

Who am I to talk about lost hope when I always have a glimpse of hope even in my darkest hour?

I strayed off topic a bit, but now I am left with these thoughts.

The red bumps on my face and hands annoy me, and likely I whine about them. But who am I to complain about suffering when I know so little of it? Who am I to judge, to compare who suffers more or less? We bear our own crosses. And who knows, the bedridden people I saw may have their own joys I know nothing about. Maybe they have accepted their fate and have found inner peace. The truth is, I don't know. What I have written about them is mostly guesswork from my own emotions that run deep within. Who am I to talk about lost hope when I always have a glimpse of hope even in my darkest hour? How am I to know how those who are seemingly blind to the light of faith and hope see the world? And do

A sister in the entrance to an upscale restaurant in Tainan

I want to find out?

Maybe the people who live long, who are sick for a long time, or who constantly need help, are not suffering, but somehow know they are indirectly giving an opportunity to others to help care for them. Could it be that some of them find not despair in their suffering, but hope because of those who choose to care for them, to look after them, and to love them despite everything? These poor, seemingly wretched people may be giving the rest of us a chance to be humble servants. Vincent DePaul, the founder of the Daughters of Charity, once wrote, "The poor are our masters." And some masters are more demanding than others.

If there was no one to love, to take care of, what would we live for?

In a way, the true poor are those who are healthy and well and who easily get distracted by worldly influences. But as I have experienced through being in touch with sick people, we are given the opportunity to reflect on ourselves, our lifestyles and purpose. If there was no one to love, to take care of, what would we live for? Ourselves, of course. But history has taught us a good lesson about being self-centered and how it always, always, leads to self-destruction. We are all "poor" in our own way, Sr. Annie said, and oftentimes it's our best gift that becomes our biggest cross. A good life is a life of humility and love; both qualities bring true happiness.

How can anyone be a great leader without first knowing how to follow? How can anyone be a good master without knowing how to serve? For many, the world often revolves around the self, *I* this, and *me* that. To the narcissistic self, the only key words are *I, me, my,* and *mine*. Tragedies can bring out the humanity in our selfish nature. Sickness and weakness can induce humility and virtue in those who are poor at heart. Some find such assertions by labeling them "religious," using it as a term of contempt. However, such a dismissal does not change the fact that the assertions are true, and I believe anyone who dismisses such important emotional, human lessons just because they have a religious feel to them (and are thus related to God, religion, saints, and so forth) is a fool.

02/27

Sister Elaine's father died tonight. Sr. Annie got the news. I was just about to take a shower when she told me. Her father was ninety-one years old and had not been well for the past few weeks. I knew his illness was part of the reason Elaine hadn't smiled recently. I haven't seen her in almost a week but she still seems close to me. The fact that Elaine and I laughed, joked, though I felt like a stranger at times around her, is still intact, even though she is sad. I sincerely hope the best for her from the bottom of my heart. I was hoping to see her smile again before I have to leave for Japan, but now I am losing that hope. I have had my three intimate girlfriends lose their fathers in the last two years, and every time I am reminded of my father who is still alive and well. Each time I hear of a father dying, I want to run into my own father's arms and never let him go. I cannot begin to imagine the pain of a daughter who has just lost her father, especially if they are best friends. I believe Elaine was close to her father, as I am with mine.

I want to console, I want to comfort, but who am I to even try when I don't understand the true nature of death, and death has not come that close to me yet?

I have seen death, as have many others, but what do we know about death? If anything is real and absolute, death is. But like many other real and profoundly disturbing things, we cannot grasp it, we cannot see it, we might not accept its finality. We see death around us all the time, taking notice sometimes and other times not even noticing. But when death turns its face towards us and snatches away what was dear to us, we just might realize our ignorance and lack of preparation for it. One moment a person is there, and in the next second—gone. All that is left is an empty shell, the frame of the picture, the box that held treasures, now emptied.

I want to console, I want to comfort, but who am I to even try when I don't understand the true nature of death, and death has not come that close to me yet? All I can do is pray and hope that those who can console will console, those who can understand, will understand, and those, like me, might in our ignorance, still serve those suffering from loss.

03/01

I have become a loyal coffee drinker since I have been in Taiwan. There are two reasons: its convenience, its price, and its taste. Okay, that was three reasons, but you get the point. I usually get what people call "city coffee." It's a new thing that the 7-Elevens are doing here, and I think it is quite a success. There are 7-Elevens at almost every corner, and they are far more convenient in Taiwan than in Japan. They offer more services and more food, which, alas, I can't eat because of my allergies. And since the 7-Elevens are everywhere, I am naturally drawn to one often. The caffé latte I buy there serves as a nice morning snack after breakfast. And even now as I write, I am sipping at my café latte, enjoying the last glances of Taitung's beautiful trees and mountainous terrain in the train home to Tainan.

Throughout my sickness, the sisters were kind to me, and I had a memorable time.

My throat hurts from trying to gag myself yesterday. I ate something again which I am allergic to. We were on our way to Toroko, a tourist spot famous for its marble mountains and rocks. Before even getting to the destination (which was about three hours from the sister's house) I became so sick to my stomach. I was still able to walk and take pictures, but my appreciation of Toroko's beauty was lost through my nausea. I felt sick to my stomach for over six hours, and the windy roads of the drive back didn't help me a bit. I felt so miserable at one point, I induced vomiting. Nothing came out and I ended up dry heaving. Probably there was nothing in my stomach by then. I drank some water to avoid becoming dehydrated. My stomach growled for food, though I still felt nauseated.

Throughout my sickness, the sisters were kind to me, and I had a memorable time. The sisters who came were Sr. Maria, Sr. Diana, and Sr. Annie. We were a cheerful bunch. We talked about all kinds of things in the car to distract me from the sick feeling. The best distraction was Sr. Annie. When we were walking through the rocky tunnels, a group of young girls and boys came walking toward us from the other side. They were mostly Taiwanese, except for one. He was a tall, skinny, fair, and red-headed boy. Sr. Annie looked at me after they passed , and said with a grin, "That boy was pretty good looking."

I, of course, had seen him, but didn't think he was handsome. He was cute, but not good-looking. So I told her, "He's okay." I didn't want to get into the whole "Who do you think is handsome?" talk with the elderly sister, but the next thing she said broke that barrier.

"Oh, yes, you like 'em dark don't you?"

I was so shocked and surprised at her quick comeback that I wanted to say something innocent. But what actually came out was "Whoa, how did you know?" We still have good laughs about that. I think the sisters know my taste in the opposite sex now: I like young men who are dark, handsome, and stout.

Yesterday nothing interesting happened until we started our drive home. It began to rain hard. The beautiful ocean I saw in the morning on the way became rough, and the dry mountains began to leak waterfalls in several places. At one point there was a large boulder in the middle of the road because of the soft dirt and all the water coming down with force. A drought followed by some occasional heavy rains is dangerous because the rains often cause huge landslides. The road we were on had several deep pools of water already and some eroded mud.

She had been with her father when he died and was speaking to him when he passed so peacefully that Elaine did not know that he was gone until the nurse came in and told her.

The sisters always pray a short prayer before each car trip, and

I'm glad they do because there are many places where we could be a victim of a landslide. I was thankful we got back in one piece that day. The rains became a bit scary.

Now I am finally back in my old room in Tainan. For the rest of the day I chilled out. I talked on Skype, checked email, and didn't see any of the sisters until dinnertime. Even then, I didn't see Elaine. Sr. Bertha told me that she was doing well. She had been with her father when he died and was speaking to him he when passed so peacefully that Elaine did not know that he was gone until the nurse came in and told her. The funeral is going to be next Monday, but only for family.

After we cleaned up for dinner, I saw Elaine sitting alone eating her dinner. Her bad posture and her solitariness made me feel pity for her. She remained silent, as did I. I wasn't sure how to start any conversation with her. Thankfully, Sr. Bertha was in the same room, so she talked to Elaine a bit. It was mostly one way though. Elaine answered, but she did not lift her eyes. I told her I learned some more Taiwanese, and she smiled slightly. But she did not look at me as she poked at her food with her chopsticks. I know there was nothing I could do to help her feel better. After all, I have only known her for the past few weeks.

03/02

Today was full. I went to art class with Sr. Annie in the morning until noon. The teacher is eighty-two years old; she speaks good English, fluent Chinese, and some Japanese. I was impressed by how quickly and easily she used these languages. I drew some bamboo, Chinese style, and plum blossoms.

When we got home for lunch, I was fatigued for some reason. I didn't do any walking and I slept like a baby last night, and yet I was terribly tired, so I took an hour nap.

I forced myself to wake up at 2:30, otherwise I probably could have slept another hour. Sr. Stella had some work for me to do, so until five o'clock I was preoccupied with folding, pasting, and cutting certain assorted paper to send out to the sponsors of this facility. It was brainless work, but it took up a lot of time, and I couldn't finish it even though I worked for about two hours. I wanted to stop the work to go see Magdalene before it got too late, but I didn't want to stop my work in the middle. I usually go see Magdalene during the early afternoons, but today it would have to be different. I went down to help with meals at five. It has been over a week since I've seen the ones who need help with eating, and I was looking forward to seeing my old girlfriend who spat out her food.

She looked good today, for she was sitting up straight for once, and both of her eyes were open. She recognized me, and actually smiled a real smile. I was happy to see her too. Her bowl of food was more mushy today so she didn't have anything to spit out. On the other hand, a lot of it just drooled down her chin instead. She usually has more solid food. I wondered if something went wrong while I was gone.

They checked her pulse and kept shouting her name to make sure she was still conscious.

After a couple of spoonfuls of liquid food, she began to wheeze. I thought it was one of her crazy sneezes, but this time it was different. Two of the nurses rushed over. They checked her pulse and kept shouting her name to make sure she was still conscious. This was happening while I sat in front of her with a bowl of her food in my hands. The nurses wandered off to other patients, but they kept an eye on her, and after that fit of wheezing, I was more careful to give her only tiny bites. Since it was so liquidy, it seemed like half of the food drained onto her bib. The nurse had checked if she had fever, too. I thought she was doing well, but I was wrong. She almost finished her whole meal, but a nurse told me to put it away. There was obviously something wrong, and all I could do was hope to see her again tomorrow.

Speaking of people who aren't doing well, the Franciscan, Sr. Helen, who always competes with the priest during rosary, is in the hospital. After her episodes of vomiting two days in a row, she threw up blood. She has been in the hospital for a few days now. The first day, she was happy and energetic; maybe she expended too much energy. She sang hymns in the hospital corridors, perhaps with the

Care facility residents listening to a musical recital

kind of high that comes before a crashing low. Sr. Bertha said she wouldn't be surprised if Sr. Helen died before the end of this week.

After bringing all the elderly people up to their floors, I went to see Magdalene. I greeted my "boyfriend" who was happy to see me, and had several pieces of newspaper articles to give me to help with studying Chinese. I hope some day I can make use of them. We made another date for tomorrow at 2:00.

Magdalene stood—she *stood*, a surprise to me since I had never before seen her standing.

I greeted the women, who all recognized me. Even those with dementia recognized me, I think, at least they smiled at me when I asked how they were doing. When I got to Magdalene's table, she wasn't there. I thought she would be in her bed, but she wasn't there either. I asked one of the old ladies who can speak more Japanese where she was. And the two of us searched for her on the second floor. We found her on the balcony. Magdalene stood—she *stood*, a surprise to me since I had never before seen her standing—with the evening breeze in her face and looking at the sisters' house with great intensity. It was obvious that she was waiting, watching for someone to come out, and I had a strange feeling that she had been waiting for me.

I joined her on the balcony, and she was surprised to see me. She didn't smile at once, and asked when I got back. I told her I got back yesterday, which was a Monday. Magdalene thought I had come home on Sunday so she was waiting for me to visit. When I assured her I came back yesterday, and had been busy since, she relaxed and smiled. I encouraged her to sit in her wheelchair, then walked her around the balcony. We went onto the larger balcony and looked up into the evening sky, both of us captivated by the way the clouds were layered, looking like a school of fish in the ocean. The sky seemed closer to me than ever. We stared up in an awed silence.

It seemed like a good idea to take her to the first floor and walk her around the yard. I hadn't seen her in ages, and I wanted to give her something different for a change. She always stays on the second floor and chooses not to go outside when everyone else goes out for walks and fresh air. Right then it was after dinner, so no one was out. I got permission from the nurses to take Magdalene out for a short walk though Magdalene wasn't enthusiastic about it because she worried about my getting tired from pushing her wheelchair. I told her I was still young and strong, and I'm used to such exercise.

I walked her around the facility, taking her to places she has never been even though she's lived here for the past two years. She told me this was only her third time to walk outside around the yard. I think I'm going to make this a habit because I could tell she enjoyed seeing the flowers up close and greeting the gardeners. Everyone knew her because she is Sr. Stella's mother.

On our walk she told me how much she missed my company and how she thought about me everyday. She asked me several times when I was leaving for Japan, and that she is saddened that she will probably never get to talk to or see me after I leave. "I can die any day, and these days I cannot read letters, and I cannot call anyone. I will miss you so much," she told me.

I will miss her too. Even in Taitung, I kept an eye out for trinkets that she would like to remember me by. I was thinking maybe a pretty bracelet or a keychain for her cell phone. I only have a few more days left in Tainan so I better hurry.

She repeated many times how she will never forget me and looked mournfully lonely when she talked of these things. I was reminded again that this person I am now seeing every day, talking to, and pushing around in her wheelchair will probably be gone soon from this world, and I won't even know it. She is still strong enough to talk and stand a little bit, but her will to live seems to be diminishing. I'd like to think I brought a spark into her everyday life that gave her initiative and motivation. And such a spark has gone both ways, for when I'm not with her I find myself thinking about when I'll have the time to see her again and what I will talk about with her. Always when I pass by her window, I look up to see if she is there.

There are several other people I have this connection with, but I don't talk to them as much as I do with Magdalene. She deserves better treatment from Sr. Stella. All Magdalene wants is conversation, company, and a little excitement in her life. I wish I could help provide that and continue our relationship until she goes.

I asked her today if once she goes to heaven, she would watch over me. She smiled and nodded. It's going to be hard saying good-bye. I am eighteen years old, and she is eighty-one. In the past few weeks I have become part of her life, and she mine. I treat her as if she were my grandmother, and she treats me like her grandchild.

03/03

I helped Sr. Annie pour pudding into the tiny cups for the snack today. She usually does this job every Wednesday and Saturday, and when I remember, I help her. Usually the pudding looks brown and smells gross, but then Taiwanese have notions different from mine about what is good. I tried tasting it once despite the smell, but still couldn't take it. Today it smelled like peaches, and looked like it would actually taste good.

He even tried to teach me some basic arithmetic, but I told him I already knew my numbers.

We had loads of clothes to fold again, but we finished before lunch. Before I knew it, it was two o'clock and time for my date. I got my notebook, some paper and pens ready and went to the second floor. I saw "boyfriend" waiting by the elevator. It's amazing how you know another person feels happy to see you. When you're with friends, you might not show it as openly as these elderly people do. He looked enthusiastic as if he anticipated some new adventure. I took him down to the first floor where we had our "class." Today it wasn't so much of a class because he told me about his home town and about old Taiwanese songs. He showed me a letter from his colleague who had written him a week ago from Japan. I think he showed this to prove he knew other people who can speak and write Japanese. He often insists on going over simple facts, ones I obviously know. But I let him do it because I know it makes him feel better. He even tried to teach me some basic arithmetic, but I told him I already knew my numbers.

When somehow we got into the topic of music, he began to write down famous old Taiwanese song titles and artists. He tried singing them too, though he couldn't carry a tune nor could I understand the words. It sounded like a chant in monotone, but I enjoyed watching him sing. He is a cute old man, bald, with brown birthmarks on his head. He has round eyes, and a big nose with crooked nostrils. When he sang, his usual bright smiley face became serious and remote. As he stared into space and chanted lines of lyrics from his youth, I couldn't help being impressed with him and with the human mind and spirit. Your body may be old, but your memory can be as fresh and clear as yesterday.

Before I could officially wrap up the lesson, Sr. Annie interrupted saying that there was someone she'd like me to meet up on the fifth floor laundry room. I told my "boyfriend" that I would come back tomorrow for another review for my Chinese, but he insisted on singing one final song before I left. I patiently listened as I cleared up the table. He had brought many snacks for me, including a can of juice which was made from a sparrow's nest. He proclaimed it to be healthy and good for beauty, though I doubted its effectiveness and was suspicious of the taste.

Finally, I took him back to his floor, then went up to the fifth floor to see who Sr. Annie wanted me to meet. He was a young man, a mere boy if you ask me. He wore a black, punky shirt with green shorts. He had jet black hair, small eyes, and occasional facial hair, some long and some short. I would not accuse him of being cute, though he spoke good English, at least, good enough for us to hold a conversation. Not as good as the yellow-tagged musician, though.

He introduced himself as Andrew, and he had a blue tag on instead of a yellow, which meant that he was a volunteer, like me, with no criminal record. I soon found out that he was a volunteer for the physical ed section of this home because he is majoring in physical therapy in a university. He is twenty years old.

We started folding laundry together, and we asked the usual introductory questions. It was almost three, rosary time, but I didn't notice when Sr. Annie left us two to go down to say the rosary for the older people.

After explaining to him my dual nationality, I asked him what nationality I looked like. I love asking these questions of people I first meet. He said I looked American. After a few minutes though, he added "You look a little Japanese, too." And when I thought this conversation was over all together, he said, "I think you are very beautiful. I presume you have a boyfriend."

Okay, first of all, I don't take compliments like this seriously. Number one, I just met him, and I believe beauty should include personality and not just looks. Secondly, he's a boy a few years older than I am. What was his intention in complimenting me like that? Was he hitting on me? These are the questions that haunt most girls who are given a random compliment by a boy. We really have no idea of the intention behind such compliments.

There was something not right about her position in the wheelchair, and as I pushed her over the brick walk, she kept sliding down until her head tilted back to face the sky.

I laughed it off, hoping there would be no more such awkward moments. Since he asked me if I had a boyfriend, I presumed he didn't have a girlfriend, so I asked. "I have a girlfriend," he said. Then I asked him if she was beautiful. He didn't answer me and instead took out his phone to show me her picture.

They had been together for about six months. Later when I asked him if he wanted to marry her someday, he said yes. The pictures of her were hard to decipher because they showed either half of her face or her face at an angle so I couldn't tell what she looked like. But I told him she was cute, anyway.

After finishing the laundry work, I went down to walk people around the yard in their wheelchairs. I haven't done this job in a while because I'm usually either doing more laundry, talking to Magdalene, or doing Sr. Stella's hands-on, brainless clerical work. By now, if I barge onto the scene, I know what to do, and the nurses are familiar enough with me not to feel compelled to give so many instructions and to trust me with everyone. I spotted my old girlfriend I used to help with meals. I called her by her name, and she lifted her head to look at me. She recognized me and smiled. I decided to take her on a walk.

There was something not right about her position in the wheelchair, and as I pushed her over the brick walk, she kept sliding down until her head tilted back to face the sky. I saw that she was staring at me. Her eyes were faded blue, and I wasn't sure if that was just because they reflected the sky or because her eyes were really that color. Did she cause herself to slide down in the chair in such an almost comical way, or was it accidental? I wheeled her back to the nurses and asked them to help her sit up again. They thanked me for watching out for her.

As one of the ladies specifically asked me to take her back to her floor, I took that as an opportunity to go see Magdalene. She sat in someone else's area, and she said that she saw me in the yard walking with the wheelchairs. I didn't know she was spying on me like that. I smiled, and asked her if she wanted to go out too, but she declined in no uncertain terms.

Today we talked about children again. She kept repeating how nightmarish it was to have four babies within five years. When I told her I wanted four children, she strongly discouraged me. I told her I wasn't planning on having one kid every year. That would be difficult. She said when she looks back to those sleepless nights because of babies crying, she gets the chills. "It scares me when I think about what I did before," she said, "but my neighbor was worse. She had sixteen children, and the family was very poor." Eight girls and eight boys, she said.

What a life. But it wasn't uncommon back then for one woman to bear more than fifteen children. It's a bit scary for me to think about. I wonder how the father felt. Living in poverty must have been so hard. I can't begin to imagine the sickness and hunger they must have experienced. It is no wonder that many families sold their daughters, a practice common within the past sixty years.

During dinnertime for the elderly folks, I again wasn't able to help my girl with her meal. The nurses specifically asked me not to feed her, and to feed the woman who usually touches her face and mumbles. She was quiet today though. The food I helped her with was still the mushy kind.

Though the woman I helped didn't mumble, she occasionally shouted random words and spat out her food almost as frequently

A festival in Taitung

as my girl used to. Some of her food splattered on my pants.

I ran back to the house after the meal because we were going out for a goodbye dinner for me. It was supposed to be a combination of three celebrations, Sr. Annie's birthday, Sr. Elaine's birthday, and my goodbye party. But since Elaine's father passed away, and Elaine never liked to celebrate her birthday anyway, it wasn't as big of a celebration as it could have been. Elaine didn't even show up.

Sr. Francesca went first, and Sr. Stella went by bicycle. Sr. Annie, Sr. Bertha and I walked to the restaurant. It was farther than we thought, and we arrived five minutes late. We were supposed to get there by six. Sr. Francesca looked pretty ticked off when we saw her. I asked her why, jokingly, and she said it was because we were late. It's only five minutes, I thought. Then I remembered what Sr. Annie had told me about Sr. Francesca. She was a complainer, and maybe being a complainer meant having mood swings as well as being generally grumpy about some things. Dealing with people being late might be one of the things that made her fussy. She looked serious and peeved for a few minutes. After a while, though, she gave up the grumpy face and started to talk animatedly.

During dinner, the sisters all thanked me for coming, and I thanked them for having me. I really enjoyed their company, though I never managed to make good connections with Sr. Francesca or Stella. I feel closer to Sr. Annie and Sr. Bertha than anyone else.

On the way back from the restaurant, we dropped by a small department store. I wasn't planning on buying anything, but I saw a beautiful black slip which I couldn't resist. It was inexpensive, too, and I always wanted a night slip for summer nights. Sr. Bertha and Sr. Annie liked it very much, too. Sr. Bertha said, "It's good to treat yourself like a lady sometimes."

So I bought it. I often wear boy shorts and a tee shirt to bed, so this was going to be a good change. Tonight, I shall sleep in my black see-through slip and feel like a princess in my simple room.

03/04

I just experienced the biggest earthquake I've felt in my life. It was only 6.0, and nothing really broke or collapsed, but it was big enough for all of us to get out of our buildings and make sure everyone was all right. The tremor lasted almost a minute from the beginning shakes through the summit of its tremble to its total immobility. I was sitting at the computer checking my email when it happened. I walked to the door while the earthquake was still happening. I pulled back though, seeing that there were glass doors, worrying they might break any moment if the quake got any worse. Immediately after the shaking stopped, there was utter silence. Though the total silence lasted only for a split second, we all felt it and listened to the nothingness after the shake. Sr. Francesca's voice came ringing, "Caroliiine!"

I walked to the door while the earthquake was still happening.

I yelled back, "I'm okay," and I grabbed my computer, and ran down stairs to go outside. I saw some of the concrete on the wall had crumbled here and there, so there was a bit of white concrete on the ground. Everything else looked normal. After waiting a moment to make sure there weren't any aftershocks, I went up the second floor.

The nurses all smiled when they saw me. Everyone was okay there. I could feel the buzz of excitement everywhere. Earthquakes may cause damage, but on a smaller scale one makes the day more interesting and exciting. I heard some sirens after the shake. There had been no news of deaths yet. I hope there are none. I went to see my "boyfriend" and the man who sits in front of me during church. They were grinning ear to ear as they told me they were fine. My "boyfriend" was waiting to take his shower. It was like nothing ever happened. I checked on Magdalene too, she was in her bed when the earthquake hit, and she was fine. We exchanged laughter of relief that nothing bad happened.

And so far the rest of the day has run like nothing unusual has happened. Of course, we talked about the earthquake during lunch and whatnot, but no one regarded it as serious. Sr. Bertha was walking when it happened, and she said she felt dizzy and almost fell before realizing that the dizziness was because of the earthquake and not because of the heat.

There is another community closer to the epicenter where several sisters live. Sr. Annie called them immediately, but they were all right also, though they suffered a bit more damage since their area got a 6.4. They said that the statue of Mary in the chapel fell and broke, and their neighbors' windows broke as well. One of the old houses was cracked so much that it will be unusable. It was old anyway, so it wasn't a major loss.

Sr. Francesca was supposed to go to Taipei by bullet train today. But all the trains were stopped for the time being because workers needed to inspect the railroad tracks to make sure there were no cracks or breaks.

That's all I know about the earthquake now. We're all thankful it happened in the morning, around 8:13, rather that at night when many are taking showers. People might have been forced to run outside naked. It might sound funny, but it's really not. I just hope this recent trend of earthquakes will stop soon. First Haiti, then Chile, and some Japan, and now Taiwan. What is up with the world now?

03/04 part 2

I cannot say exactly how I have changed; I just have.

When you are thrown into another world, another culture, you often see yourself in another kind of mirror. You see yourself through the eyes of strangers and feel their pain of living. I now not only view everything from a slightly different perspective, but more important is how I view myself as changed during the past month. I cannot say exactly how I have changed; I just have. Upon arriving in Taiwan, I was thrown into a world full of aged people and illness, a world where people live in close community and practice daily religious rituals. I have developed deep friendships and simple connections which I will cherish for the rest of my life, ones that can never be repeated.

At first, my fuel to wake up every morning came from the hunger for breakfast and the necessity to be at Mass. Now I am fueled by the people themselves, their smiles mostly and voices of encouragement and by their efforts to live well. I have grown so accustomed to communicating in facial and physical action that sometimes I think I now communicate better without words.

As suddenly as I was thrown into this beautiful world of old age and wisdom, I will just as suddenly take leave of it. I was expecting to stay in Tainan with the laundry, the old people, including my boyfriend, Magdalene, and the rest of the gang until Monday. But today, Thursday, Sr. Annie told me that plans changed, and that I was to leave the next morning at 8:30. I was honestly disappointed and excited. True, I was to go to another community and for what could be exciting new experiences, but I wasn't ready to let go of a community I finally understood somewhat. I had just finished helping with a meal when I got the news, and I was feeling great because I got to help my old girlfriend again, though I swear her food was just like sticky soup.

For me, working with the aged was a difficult business to get into, but it's even harder to pull out.

Anyhow, the first reaction when I heard the news from Sr. Annie was to run to get my camera and go to the second floor where the people knew me best. I stopped by each man and woman I always greet who had lightened up my day with smiles and simple conversation. I told them I was leaving tomorrow and not coming back. I have heard this phrase many times in classical novels and movies. But it is lonesome to actually have to say the phrase, knowing that there will be no happy endings as in books or movies. Most of them looked sad, and one woman tried to tell me I would come back someday. I hope so, but I'm not sure anyone I know now will be alive when I have the chance to come back.

For me, working with the aged was a difficult business to get into, but it's even harder to pull out. That's because deep down I know that these people have not much time left in this world, so I naturally want to make their stay here a better one, and if it means visiting with them everyday, showing that they mean something to me, then that's good, and it's neither difficult nor a sacrifice.

I tried giving her my bracelet with my name on it, but she kept refusing it saying that she will cry every time she sees it.

I took pictures, and my boyfriend said that he has treated me as the granddaughter he never had, that he will think of me forever that way. Remembering what he said makes me tear up. He never had his own grandchild, and my Japanese grandfather was a distant man. What an honor and privilege I've had to be involved in these people's lives, though it was only for a short time. I thought of him as my grandpa too, and Magdalene and Bertha as my grandmothers.

I saved visiting Magdalene to the last. But when I went her bedroom, she wasn't there. I guessed that she was out again at the balcony, and I was right. She stood, staring into nothingness. I hugged her and felt awkward about it since she wasn't used to hugging.

We stood on the balcony under the great pink sun-setting sky and talked of the future. I told her that I had to leave the next day, and I could see the happiness drain from her face. I tried giving her my bracelet with my name on it, but she kept refusing it saying that she will cry every time she sees it. She pouted her lips and said she will miss me everyday so much. She said so many things to me that I will treasure in my heart and keep to myself. She gave me a glimpse of how some people saw me. Magdalene said there are people who look ugly, not in the face, but an aura they have that is either unfriendly or hostile. She said when people see me, they see happiness and beauty. She had frequently told me how nice I look but this time she said more. It's not the face where true beauty lies, she said, but the heart.

She gave me advice about raising children and proclaimed that all throughout the hardships of bringing up her four children, she had not once beaten any one of them, though her husband did on multiple occasions. She told me that whomever I marry will be a lucky man and told me to find a suitor who won't make me cry.

Magdalene said that she might die any time now, and I told her again to think of me and watch over me in heaven. I know she will remember to do that. I said I will see her again some day, but not in this world. She nodded, and we looked into the evening sky again.

Later, during my last supper with the sisters in Tainan, Sr. Stella thanked me for boosting her mother's self-image. I didn't know what she meant at first, but apparently Magdalene does not really think highly of herself since she did not have a good education because she was the twelfth child in her family. She could not read or write until after she was in her forties, and she felt insecure living on a floor with so many educated women. After I came along, everyone was surprised that she could communicate with me and have appointments with me everyday. Now, Sr. Stella said, her mother's nosey neighbors won't be so condescending, and Magdalene has something to pride herself on.

I gave Magdalene a couple more hugs and said my farewell and told her to be at the window so I could wave goodbye.

Packing was a nightmare. Since I had been planning to leave this area in a few days instead of tomorrow, my room was a mess. I had received many gifts and bought some items, so I had to leave some of my old clothes behind in order to fit everything in my suitcases. Both of my suitcases were stuffed even after sacrificing some favorite shirts and underwear.

It didn't feel like I would be leaving there the next day. I couldn't get to sleep, so I turned on some slow Chinese music, which unfortunately, made me think of death. Before I knew it, though, it was morning.

03/05

Since I did all my major packing yesterday, I just had to put up the last minute pajamas and facial creams normally used in the morning. Still, it felt like the start of another day except for the suitcases reminding me that this new day will end with another bed, another place, another room. I have become so cozy here and everywhere in Tainan. I will leave part of myself here as I did when leaving the Philippines. But it is also true that a part of this place will stay with me.

I am on the bus as I write this, going to Taipei. The bus costs about one third the price of taking a train. Surprisingly though, the buses are cleaner and have bigger seats than the train, and the travel time is about the same. Since a couple of years ago when martial law was lifted, bus companies have had more competition because they are no longer owned by the government. Such competition makes services better and better.

Do I really want to come back to find some of them dead and to see others all grown old and slow?

I'm not sure what my plan is going to be for the weekend. I'm supposed to go to Touchung, another community in the north of Taipei where there is also a small home for the elderly. I heard it was as beautiful as Taitung, so I am looking forward to it. Sr. Annie said that the sisters there have planned my whole two days stay, and I will be doing some work as well. I hope they don't expect more than I can deliver because I so hate to disappoint.

I said my last goodbyes to Sr. Francesca today in Taipei. She had gone ahead for a counsel meeting. I gave her a couple of hugs. Though I didn't get as close to her as I might have, I will still miss her face and company. She kept telling me I will see her again someday, a statement that reminded me of my conflicted feelings about returning to Taiwan. It would be great again to see the sisters and other people I have come to care so much about, but it will be a couple of years before I'll have an opportunity to return, and if I do return, I'm not sure if I'll be ready to see the changes in them. They are all old, and though Sr. Annie is only going to be fifty this year, others like Sr. Bertha whom I have come to love will be in their late seventies or early eighties. I will probably never see Sr. Bertha as happy and strong as I saw her this morning. Do I really want to come back to find some of them dead and to see others all grown old and slow? All fragile and dull? I don't know if I can handle such changes. I'm being selfish and self-protective, I know.

As soon as we dropped by the community in Taipei, I was off to another community up in Touchung with Sr. Annie and Sr. Edith, another Filipino sister who is the Sister Servant of the community in Touchung. It was on the east side of Taiwan like Taitung, but up north. On the train I didn't get to sit next to the sisters. We all sat separately, and I sat next to a college student who was working on his laptop. The scenery was mostly mountains and some ocean. It was cloudy so it wasn't so beautiful.

There were two new sisters I was introduced to when I arrived around 5:30 in the afternoon. One was Vietnamese, another Sr. Maria, and the other was an American from Chicago. Her name is Sr. Martha, and I never expected her to be so plump and white. The first time I saw her, I thought she wore an abundance of white make up. She was pale and had washed blue eyes. She wasn't as outgoing as Sr. Annie, but she had a quiet kind of sense of humor which got people laughing. She cooked dinner for us. Since it's a Friday in Lent, there was no meat. Personally, giving up meat isn't any kind of penance for me because I love vegetables. Tonight's meal included mashed potatoes and corn soup. My favorites.

For the first time I was to sleep in a separate building from the sisters. In Touchung the Daughters of Charity also own a home for the elderly, but a much smaller one that can accommodate only twenty people. I visited the building and found it old and worn, so on the outside it looked abandoned. It was dark inside too, which created an atmosphere I didn't much care for, but the nurses I met seemed both competent and friendly. In Tainan, the nurses were too busy with their own schedules to interact much with me, but I think here they will actually take time with me so I can help them out and they will not relegate me to doing laundry. I will find out tomorrow because I'm supposed to spend a day at the home. I feared I might conclude that I'd seen enough older people, but I didn't. We're all going to grow old some day.

The first impression of the room I am staying in was a good one. It had a TV, the walls were light blue, and I had my own bathroom separate from the shower. I even had access to a washing machine. But when I actually stayed in the room and showered, I wished to be back in my old room in Tainan. True, the shower was separated from the toilet for once, but I think whoever used that room before was a heavy smoker. There was only one cigarette butt on the floor, but the whole shower room was covered with an unpleasant yellow film from burning tobacco. I am so glad I wore my sandals into the shower. The place stank of cigarettes. The windows didn't have screens on them, and I feared people outside might see me. The administrator who set me up in this room assured me that no one could see in, but I think some creep who used a little ingenuity could easily find a place where he could see into the shower room. Also, the lights were too white to suit me.

> **The bittersweetness of time haunts me even as I am now uneasy and uncomfortable in my new room.**

I miss Tainan already and Sr. Bertha and Sr. Stella and Sr. Elaine and all the people. I want to see them again, but like I said, I want to remember them as I do now, and change is already underway for all of us, especially Bertha. She is small and strong now, but she is not so young at sixty-nine. She has almost all white hair. Paula already has the first symptoms of Alzheimer's, and Sr. Annie will soon finish her thirty years in Taiwan, so she will go back to the U.S. where she will stay for the rest of her life. The bittersweetness of time haunts me even as I am now uneasy and uncomfortable in my new room.

My moving often, being pulled from one place and thrust into another while trying to grasp the enormity of huge changes, and knowing I need to fit into new surroundings strikes me like trying to fit my right foot into my left shoe. It's my shoe, but it just doesn't feel comfortable. Every time I see my reflection in a mirror I remember the way I looked in other mirrors elsewhere: mirrors in the Philippines where I spent my Christmas holidays last year, mirrors in Tainan and in the U.S., mirrors that held an image of the girl Caroline as she was then, as she felt in those other places and times when I woke up and went to sleep in different rooms. If I'm not careful, I can feel lost in my own reflection here in this new place in Taiwan. But it's not vanity, peering at myself in this new mirror, because when I see myself now, here in my new and less than comfortable surroundings, I don't see any absolute *me*, for my image is clouded by other perceptions of this face and this emotional being.

Somehow I've always thought I would come back to places I've visited and to good people I've met even while knowing the impossibility of always returning. But now a realization of the possible finality of my visit to Taiwan hits me stronger than ever. I don't know if I will ever see the sisters again, and I do know that I will never see most of the old people again unless I come back within a year or two. Even then I know there will be many missing faces.

Right now I want the night to be over so I can go out and do something in the morning. Thankfully, I am staying here only three nights. In the morning there will be only two more to go.

03/06

I could not sleep until one o'clock this morning, possibly because I had coffee to drink in the late afternoon. I woke up early as usual and went to the sister's house for breakfast, since Mass is at eight o'clock here.

During breakfast Sr. Martha told me about the reality of migrant workers and their suffering. It all started with her telling us her plan to visit migrants in a prison. I asked her why they were in prison, and she explained in detail how migrant workers came to be and how many of them end up in prison.

In Asia many countries such as Japan, Korea, Singapore, Malaysia, and China are now accepting migrant workers. The workers are mostly sent from the Philippines, Vietnam, Indonesia, and other less wealthy countries. The workers usually go through a broker who gets them jobs and visas in a country foreign to the workers. It is possible to become a migrant worker without going through a broker, but the migrant must have good connections in another country, people willing to go to several government offices to fill out many forms. Since most migrant workers have no such connections, they go to a broker. The broker can easily find jobs for them at low wages, but he will charge about five thousand American dollars for his services.

In Taiwan, the minimum wage for a month is about six hundred American dollars, and the broker takes seventy-five dollars monthly until the five thousand is paid off. Workers have expenses such as rent and food, so it will take them a couple of years before they can send money back to their families who need it desperately. These migrant workers are usually caregivers or housemaids in different households. They work long hours seven days each week, and are willing to do so because they so need employment. Brokers are often cruel to the migrant workers. Typically a broker brings in tens of migrant workers at a time, so if he gets seventy-five dollars a month from each worker, he soon makes plenty of money. Some brokers deal in illegal human trafficking, forcing workers into prostitution.

If police catch workers who have broken their original work contracts, the workers go to jail.

After some months of barely earning a living, workers are vulnerable to illegal offers of other jobs where the pay is better. Many migrant workers run away to take new jobs, and often the previous employers threaten to take away their passports, though it is illegal to take anyone's passport away. If police catch workers who have broken their original work contracts, the workers go to jail. After a few months in prison, the workers are sent home, and they are made to pay fines and for passage back to their own countries.

These migrant workers are not bad people, Sr. Martha said. They're not criminals. They're people wanting to work and to earn money for their families. It's the brokers, Sr. Martha believes, as well as the businessmen who shamelessly abuse these workers, who should be punished. There have been several court cases because the migrant workers have been so mistreated and made to pay more money than required by law.

On the topic of prostitution and human trafficking, Sr. Martha said that the Daughters of Charity used to help girls who were forced into prostitution. In the past unscrupulous men lured from their rural homes many beauties among Taiwanese aborigines. The men claimed to take the girls into cities to help them with education, but they were actually selling their bodies. These girls were victimized, lied to and tricked, and the Daughters of Charity worked to rescue them. But that was years ago, and now the story has changed. The girls on the street these days are locals, Sr. Martha said, and they are there voluntarily, as high school and college students trying to earn extra money. The Daughters of Charity have no work there since the girls choose prostitution of their own free will.

The Mass was bilingual: Mandarin and Taiwanese. The priest came from Holland, and he looked so old that he could crumble at any moment. He was fluent in Taiwanese. I have become acquainted with the difference between Taiwanese and Mandarin, and now can tell the difference when I hear them. Taiwanese has similar pronunciations to the Japanese characters more than does Mandarin. But generally Taiwanese sounds bouncy, and Mandarin is more smooth and like a song. I believe Taiwanese has five tones, while Mandarin has only four. At first I had no idea what the people were saying when they spoke Taiwanese.

During the early morning, I met the elderly people. Unlike the ones in Tainan, they are, in general, more aware, and most of them can take care of themselves. Some of them are in wheelchairs but are much more alert and talkative. I spoke in Japanese with some, and they are glad to hear it though most of the time they respond in Mandarin or Taiwanese.

This morning, Sr. Martha had catechism with two little girls. I played with them outside for a while. They were both nine years old, and they liked being helpful with the old people. Sr. Martha made each a card where she put a sticker every time one of them did something helpful around the home. So these two girls run all over the place, giving cookies to the elderly, helping them stand up, and sometimes bringing people wildflowers from outside. The folks know and like these little girls, and one of the older men tried to play tag with them because he could still walk. He had a cagey, playful look on his face, and he often tried to reach out to catch one of the girls as she passed by. He did that with me, too.

I talked to the girls in Mandarin, and we got along pretty well. I could understand most of what they said, and they understood me. I realize I'm not bad at small talk now, and if I had chosen to stay even a couple more months longer in Taiwan, I could probably have become pretty fluent in Mandarin. Mass helps a lot because there is much repetition, and I hear certain words everyday so they stick quickly. And with the elderly there is much repetition also, for I must repeat directions and words often for those hard of hearing. I pick up Taiwanese words like that as well.

After class Sr. Annie and I took a walk to the beach. It was foggy at first when we got to the beach so we saw little of the ocean. But the waves were big, loud, and powerful, so in spite of the fog, the scene had a primordial grandeur to it. There must have been a typhoon somewhere in the sea because huge waves pounded the beach. I could have stayed there forever just watching the waves appearing out of the fog and tumbling onto the shore with loud crashes. We stayed awhile just staring. As usual, Sr. Annie had loads of stories to tell, but I still had some peaceful moments with the ocean. I wish I could take my computer there and write while listening to the waves and feeling the wind in my face.

For lunch I had a type of vegetable that I wish to find again in Japan if that's possible. I do not know its English name, but it consisted of green leaves with purple juice. It is a bit slimy and has a purple root underground. When you sauté the green leaves, they produce a beautiful lavender liquid. I put it on rice, so I can say I ate purple rice.

03/08

I have not been in the mood to write for a few days. As the dates in this journal indicate, I have missed a couple of days. So much has happened, so much has been burned into my memory, yet I cannot get myself to write any of it down. Maybe the memories are to be forever only in my mind. I know I will regret not writing these few things down before I close this journal for good. So I am writing now, back in the room I started with when I first arrived in Taiwan. I have itchy eyes, and a red nose from the new allergy I have with some of the plants here.

Today I arrived here in Taipei around noon with Sr. Annie and Sr. Maria, one of the Vietnamese sisters from Touchung. We arrived on a fancy bus. The buses here in Taiwan have the feel of airplanes because of the high ceilings airplane-like seating. Coming from Taipei to Touchung by train took an hour and thirty minutes. By bus, going through several dozen new tunnels, it only took forty minutes. Sr. Annie was quiet almost the entire trip, which is not unusual, since I had my iPod on, and she usually doesn't talk on trips like this. I think she knows how her voice carries sometimes, or maybe she just likes to enjoy the scenery.

Yesterday was a Sunday, and it was an eventful day. I spent some time with one of the local boys whose English name was Vincent and who had just turned seventeen. He was an accomplished drummer because he had been taking lessons since the fifth grade. He stands 185 cm tall (about 6 feet one inch) and is slender, but not skinny, has a dark complexion, and some may call him handsome. I was supposed to teach him English by listening to him read a novel, but we ended up discussing music and talking in general. His English is good enough for me to speak pretty fast, and he can still understand. His dream is to go to a good university in Boston to study music and become a better drummer.

After I listened to him play his drums with such passion and talent, I wouldn't be surprised if he focused only on music during his studies.

Sr. Martha had set me up with him because she wanted me to talk him into taking another path with his education or maybe just examine many possibilities before focusing on one subject. That's what I planned to do. I tried to explain that a university is a place to expand his knowledge. He already knows a lot about music, especially drumming, but he hasn't explored other areas of knowledge. I told him if he can go to a university before going into vocational school, he would get a better look at the world and have a chance to see other options for his future. He nodded the whole time I talked, but I don't know how much of it he truly heard. After I listened to him play his drums with such passion and talent, I wouldn't be surprised if he focused only on music during his studies.

I ate lunch with his family, and then he took me to a famous ice cream shop. After that we biked to the beach where we drank coffee at a fancy coffee shop. Some may call it a date, given what we did and the places we went. There were real couples everywhere, but I don't think either of us considered our being together to be a date. We just met each other, and he was younger than I by far. He was a good young man though, and as he grows up, I hope he keeps his gentlmanly character and his reserved manners.

After I returned from my outing with Vincent, I suggested that Sr. Annie and I take a walk around the mountains since we had recently gone to the ocean. She was up for it, as usual. She loves walking as much as I do, and she walks longer distances than I sometimes, something that surprises me since she is seventy-six years old.

Our walk was magnificent. We walked beside mountains and streams, by old and new homes, and by the rice fields and vegetable gardens. As part of our adventure, we went into a rural police station for the bathroom. The police officer, a young man, was watching TV when we arrived, and he was clearly startled, though I think we made his day. Two foreigners dropping by for a bathroom stop must have been an unusual event for him. I'll bet he went home and told his wife, if he has one.

We walked about six miles, and we came back just in time for dinner. Sr. Annie's knees have been bothering her since we got to Touchung, but I think the walk did her good. We had no way of knowing that the walk would be her last for a long time.

We arrived in Taipei around noon today. Sr. Maria had her classes to go to in another area so she left us to take another bus. I had my bags with me, and I helped Sr. Annie carry her bags since she had two and one of them was filled with books. I had a lot on me already, but it felt good to help Sr. Maria.

In Touchung there was not even a McDonald's since it was such a rural and isolated place. Worse, there was no Starbucks. Sr. Annie knows how much I love the green tea drinks there, and after I took her to Starbucks a couple of times in other places, I think she became hooked on one of the drinks. We passed a Starbucks immediately after leaving the bus station, and decided we would have our lunch there.

Neither of us was hungry since we had a big breakfast, so it was a simple meal. She talked a lot as usual. If I ever said that her talking bored me, I sincerely take it back. Now that I know her better I much look forward to her bursts of consecutive stories. All of them are either about her past, her friends' past, or her family's past. Recently most have been comical stories, and we end up laughing a great deal. I would love to write some down, and even Sr. Annie had admitted that other friends of hers had told her to write a book on her tales. "But I'm more of a talker than a writer," she told me.

We stepped out of the café, and that's when things went downhill.

"And I'm more of a writer than a talker," I said.

But I think it won't do her stories justice if I write them, for her stories rely so much on her intonation, timing, and gestures for their effect. During our Starbucks lunch she was in her best and most comical storytelling form.

That area of the city was unfamiliar to Sr. Annie, so we planned to explore it for the rest of the day before we had to go back to the Provincial House in the upper city. We were all ready to go window shopping, and I felt ready to spend some money. We stepped out of the café, and that's when things went downhill.

Poor Sr. Annie, with her double-lens glasses, didn't see that there were two small steps going down from the Starbucks to the road. In a split second she was half on the floor, though I managed to catch her to keep her from falling on her face. In that instant, all joy and happiness drained from her face, and she limped to the wall. I knew something really bad had happened, and I worked at holding her upright.

"I twisted my knee when I went down," she said, then produced a small bottle of green oil, which she rubbed on her knee. "That helps some," she said.

I remembered that her knee had been bothering her before she tripped. Now it gave her such pain that she could now hardly put any weight on it. Sr. Annie is not a woman to complain so she said only, "We're going to have to take a cab."

I supported her in a slow shuffle to the road where we called a cab. She bit her lip in silence, and when I asked how bad her foot hurt on a scale of 1 to 10, she didn't answer at first. The pain appeared to come in waves each time she put some weight on her injured leg.

I carried two bags, and held her arm, and pulled some luggage on wheels. It was good to be able to help her, though I feel some guilt for her pain because of my introducing her to Starbucks. True, it was her idea to eat lunch there today, but still, I was the one who introduced her to Starbucks in the first place.

I flagged down a cab that had just dropped off some clients, and I helped Sr. Annie into the car. "You've certainly done your job in assisting an elderly person today," she said, then thanked me. I know she meant it because if I wasn't here, her accident would have been much worse. Then again, if I wasn't here, perhaps it wouldn't have happened at all.

Her knee was worse than I had feared. Before getting better, it got worse. Since most of the sisters in Taipei are nurses, they tried figuring out what was best for her. Her leg wasn't swollen, so it was probably the tendons or the muscle. They are going to try to take her to the doctor tomorrow. Meanwhile she spent the rest of the day in a wheelchair or in bed, since she cannot walk. Ironic how things work: I pushed wheelchairs in Tainan, Taichung, and now I push one for my dear friend in Taipei. She said, "God let this happen for a reason. I am going to offer this pain up for Elaine who's having her father buried today."

I could still see and hear her disappointment in how things turned out. We had looked forward to visiting places in Taipei together. Now she can't even walk to the bathroom without some help.

If the weather will allow me to take Sr. Annie on a walk by pushing her wheelchair, I would much like to do so. I am the strongest woman here, and I can handle some muscle work. And she'd enjoy it too. I still want to hear more stories, and see more of the city with her before I leave. One of the sisters here also promised to take me out, but she is essentially a stranger and very quiet, so I can't be myself around her as I can with Sr. Annie.

I hear it raining now. It's almost eleven at night, and I haven't had a decent sleep in a couple of days. I hope tomorrow will bring a better adventure, for today's ended as a sad one.

03/09

I went to sleep with the sound of rain and awakened to the sound of rain. It's a peaceful sound, though I wasn't enthused about it knowing I have to walk in the cold rain to go to church. In Taipei, unlike other houses, they do not hold Mass in the chapel every morning, but in the church, which is about a five minute walk from the house. I caught one of the cars going to the church so I didn't get too wet. It was a gloomy morning, and I was correct to expect a fairly slow and gloomy day.

Sr. Annie didn't leave her room until breakfast, so I sat alone during Mass. It was all right I guess. I'm used to such isolation now, and I understand more than I did when I was here two months ago.

This morning my mood has been pretty low. I have mood swings once in a while that make everything turn black. Today I sank some because I have a list of items I have to buy before leaving Taipei. A gray, cold rain fell, Sr. Annie wasn't moving, and I wasn't sure who might go shopping with me. However, it wasn't lack of a shopping companion that bothered me so much as the rain. If the sun were out, I wouldn't have minded going by myself to explore the city since the house is in the middle of a huge metropolis. But with cold, dreary rain? I longed for the summery Tainan weather.

The wet, limp day reminded me again how lucky I was to have stayed in Tainan for so long. I had learned to wander around Tainan without feeling lost. And, of course, I had Sr. Annie and Sr. Bertha, and others who took good care of me. Here I felt that useless feeling creeping up again. But I pushed it away telling myself that I'll be home in Japan in a few days, and then I will miss much about Taiwan. University applications and essays for scholarship committees to ponder awaited in my room in Japan. I didn't look forward to that.

There are many sisters here since this is the Provincial House.

They were the ones whom I met first right after arriving in Taiwan. I hadn't even begun to take my journal until I arrived in Tainan, so I haven't written anything about the sisters in Taipei. But then I don't have much to tell because I don't know these sisters' names that well, and I sometimes confuse their faces.

It's a good thing she smiles a lot because when she doesn't smile, she looks pretty scary.

First, there is Sr. Susanna who is a genuine Texan. She is the one I contacted from Japan in planning the trip here. She is a large woman with a moon-round face, big hips, huge bottom, and white hair. She loves meat, Tex-Mex food, and she likes to stereotype everything and anything. My first impression of her was a good one, but she became increasingly judgmental. "Japanese people," she told me with an air of certainty and superiority, "always put seaweed and fish in everything!"

Her statement and demeanor felt like a challenge, so I said, "What about the food in Taiwan? Everything people eat here has soy and peanuts in it." Neither her generalization nor mine is true, of course, Her voice is high-pitched, too. It's a good thing she smiles a lot because when she doesn't smile, she looks pretty scary.

I remained silent through breakfast reflecting on the fact that few of the sisters here are bubbly and energetic like those in the other houses.

There's Sr. Rose, who is actually the Sister Servant of Liogue, one community I never got to visit. Because she had heart surgery within the past few months, she has to stay here until she is completely healed. She is a quiet woman, so I can't say much about her. She appears Filipino because of her dark skin, but I think she might actually be completely Taiwanese.

There's Sr. Magdalene, with whom I thought I had a connection in my first arrival. She is Chinese, and she works as a secretary and a translator for this house. She translates Chinese, French, and English. On my arrival she taught me some origins of the Chinese character and was kind to me. She is still kind, but I noticed she seems a bit distant, that she now seems less outgoing. I believe she is more a silent server than anything else. She will be the one who will take me to the night markets and places I want to go tomorrow.

There's Sr. Olivia, an American woman who used to be 5'9" but now is about my height due to her osteoporosis. She is apparently the resident genius among the sisters here, since she has been a professor of English as well as other things I can't remember now. At eighty years old she still conducts classes. I see her playing games on the computer a lot in the evenings. Mostly she plays Scrabble and games related to words. She must really love her job.

There are more American sisters here than in the other communities I have visited. One other, whose name is also Sr. Olivia, though we add "Lawson" (her last name) at the end of her name to distinguish between the Olivias, instead of calling them the tall Olivia and the short Olivia. Sr. Olivia Lawson took me shopping today for things that my mother had requested last minute. There are more sisters in the house of course, but I know too little of them to mention them here.

Sr. Olivia Lawson took me to a store that carries handcrafted Taiwanese gifts. It was a beautiful place, and most of its merchandise was above affordability. But it was *hao-kan* as the Chinese say, meaning "nice to look at." I found the items that I needed to buy for other people. She took me to the underground malls where I bought myself some cute tights. They were made in Japan, but they cost less here than in Osaka.

We ate at Starbucks for lunch. I had a blueberry bagel which must have contained something I was allergic to because I spent the rest of the day having waves of odd stomach problems. Sr. Olivia enjoys Starbucks too, and she had a cinnamon roll for her lunch.

We returned after lunch because she had made a doctor's appointment at the Veteran's hospital for Sr. Annie's knee. The hospital reopened at 1:30. We aimed at getting there around 2:45.

I have never been in a major hospital in Taiwan till now. Observing the business of the hospital reminded me why I don't like hospitals. I once stayed in a big hospital like this as a child for two weeks because I had a stomach problem that no doctor could figure out; it was a hospital that didn't seem so terrible at the time. But this one was downright gloomy in spite of all the glaring white lights.

There were long lines and doors which looked as if they could open to prison cells.

While waiting I explored a book and occasionally people-watched. A man sitting near me sneezed a lot, and I hoped he wasn't spewing contagious viruses all over the room.

Finally, our number was called, and we went through one of the prison cell doors, a heavy, large one. The doctor looked young, and he spoke pretty good English. He said it was most likely a muscle sprain and Sr. Annie will be normal in about two weeks. He ordered an X-ray to make sure his diagnosis was right. It was, and he prescribed some medication for pain and some for enhancing development.

This time her kindness and enthusiasm seemed somehow forced and superficial.

I pushed Sr. Annie back down to the roundabout or traffic circle in front of the hospital to wait for a taxi where we saw a migrant caregiver attending a woman who sat paralyzed in a wheelchair and had tubes all about her. The caregiver looked Filipina. As our eyes met she smiled. She asked me if I were Filipina. She probably thought I was a caregiver for Sr. Annie.

The rest of the day proved to be slow and dull, though I got to go to the night market with Sr. Magdalene, the one who was so kind to me when I first arrived in Taiwan. This time her kindness and enthusiasm seemed somehow forced and superficial. She is a good woman, but sometimes she has a sharp temper. One morning she got upset because while she was trying to sleep, some sisters were talking in the next room. She marched into the room, and said, "Can you two be quiet? I'm trying to sleep here."

Sr. Magdalene used to be a teacher, and she worked both with children and the old people. I know she is hardworking and good-hearted, yet still she scares me a little. I may be just overanalyzing. But one thing now feels certain: that I would never have gotten so close to her, even if I spent a whole month with her.

3/10

Today was a day for movies and last minute sightseeing. I began the animated *Ice Age* with Sr. Annie in the morning after Sr. Magdalene cleaned up my eyebrows. When I say "cleaned up," I use a local term for removing facial hair. Taiwanese do this by just using one line of string. I mentioned wanting to try it before I left, and Sr. Magdalene told me last night that she knows how to use the string, and that way I wouldn't have to spend money. I felt grateful, but I wanted to go to those ladies on the street because they have been cleaning up faces for years, so I figured they would be more professional and maybe less painful. But how could I say that when Sr. Magdalene was so pushy about the matter? I let her do it.

It turned out okay because she taught me how to use the string on my own face. It was more simple than I had thought, and more painful. It looks easy and comfortable, but I'll guarantee it's not without pain. So I now have "baby skin," along with knowledge of a new kind of pain. Sr. Magdalene reminded me of a Chinese saying: "If you want to stay beautiful, you have to put up with pain."

Sr. Olivia asked me in the morning if I wanted to do anything else here in Taipei. I mentioned the 101 building, the second tallest building in the world only second to the one recently built in Dubai. She seemed enthusiastic about going, and today was more sunny so the view should be a good one. She had to do some errands, so while I waited I watched the movie with Sr. Annie. She felt much better today, and she needed only a cane, not a wheelchair.

Sr. Olivia arrived ready to go and with news that Sr. Susanna will join us. I didn't mind, of course, but with her weight and bad knees it might restrict us some, and likely we would go to the 101 Building and coming straight back. I was right.

The transportation system in Taipei is amazing in its efficiency and price. Although the roads are bumpy and crowded, and though in the bus I feel like I will be in a major accident any moment, everything is inexpensive and convenient. A bus arrives every few minutes at every station, and you can go all over town. You can buy a card to use within the city for any transportation system except taxis. Taxis aren't so expensive either, so people make frequent use of them. It was a bit scary watching Sr. Susanna huff and puff up and down steep bus steps. When we walked she was always lagging behind. Sr. Olivia, being a very fast walker since she was young, always zipped ahead, and I worked at following her. Sr. Susanna was without a doubt twice as slow, so we frequently had to wait for her.

It took longer than I thought to go to the 101 Building. You could see it from afar, but the distance was greater than it looked. We took two different buses and two different train lines. They are all so convenient and easy that after a few days, I could probably go wherever I want in the city. But I'm going back to Japan tomorrow.

We got to the 101 Building finally and walked, shopping on the first five floors where all the brand name clothing stores were. We spent much time in the bookstore, and I realized that though I pride myself in being wellread, I'm really an amateur. Olivia not only knew the old classics, she had read many modern books I am not familiar with. I knew several details about classic authors, but I had never heard of many of the modern writers. I felt a bit silly standing in such ignorance among all those books with a woman who knew almost every author and book in the store.

I wanted to go all the way up to the top of Building 101, but Sr. Olivia said she would not. I asked her if she was afraid of heights, but she wouldn't say. So I guessed that going up would be pricey, which it was. I paid for myself and Sr. Susanna.

The elevator was supposed to be the fastest in the world. It went up to the ninety-first floor in about thirty seconds. My eyes felt as if they might pop from the changes in pressure. There were no windows inside the elevator, which I thought was a stupid thing. What's the fun of going up the fastest elevator in the world on one of the tallest buildings in the world when there is no view from the elevator?

The guides spoke three languages, first English, then Japanese, and then Chinese. They were much better with English than Japanese. I think Japanese can be spoken if one studies, but it is almost impossible for a foreigner to speak Japanese without a heavy accent. I certainly don't speak perfect Japanese, though I've heard it since birth and spent seven years in a Japanese school. I remember still my friends poking fun at my Japanese because they claimed it sounded funny.

I have been to the top of several big towers like the Tokyo tower, so I'm used to high places. This Building 101 showed us much beauty, and it was fun seeing the city from such a high point. I took several pictures. The cars looked smaller than toy cars, and we were higher than some of the surrounding mountains. The weather was overcast, so I couldn't see as well as I probably could have on a better day, but with so much pollution in the city, the view we had that day might well be the best anyone could see on any day.

Everything to her is either unreal, negative, or stereotyped in bad ways, and she is far too generous with her negative opinions.

To conclude our adventures, we went to a Starbucks in the building. I had my green tea, of course. While we sat with our drinks, I got to observe Sr. Susanna more. She loved to talk, and she was friendly and smiley when she did, but when it came to listening, she put on a more serious face. Some might say it was a face of indifference. As Sr. Olivia blabbed away about how frustrating the computer can be, Sr. Susanna stared at her coffee cup and occasion-ally nodded. Sometimes she was silent for such a long time that I wasn't sure if she was listening.

I showed her my green tea drink, with it's beautiful milky green color. Immediately Sr. Susanna said, "That's food coloring all right."

Okay sister, I thought. You asked for it. I explained to her that the green in my cup came from the type of tea and that sometimes the green got darker. Maybe, I admitted only to myself, it did have food coloring, but I will not believe it. It's my favorite drink in the world, and I wouldn't have someone dissing its beautiful color. Sr. Olivia spoke up in defense of the tea because she also likes it.

I found myself wishing Sr. Susanna would stop being so judgmental. Everything to her is either unreal, negative, or stereotyped in bad ways, and she is far too generous with her negative opinions. I did, though, find out later that Sr. Susanna has a deeper, kinder side to her that I could not readily see.

At night I felt the excitement of going home. I have had my yearnings for home locked inside me for too long so I won't slide into depression from homesickness. I let those feelings loose now, and I became giddy with excitement.

Since the Sister Servants' meeting was on the day of my departure, some of the Sister Servants whom I have come to know arrived here today, and I got to catch up with them some. Sr. Edith came, and we spoke some Tagalog and exchanged laughs.

Sr. Jane, who is a Sister Servant of Liogue, the only community I have not been able to go to, came around eight at night. I was glad to see her, since she was one of my favorite American sisters. She is an extrovert, and very talkative. Even the talkative Sr. Annie becomes a quiet listener around her. Though her voice is weaker and quieter than Annie's, she talks more smoothly and eloquently than Sr. Annie, and likes to talk and walk at the same time. Sr. Annie prefers to stop every time she makes a significant or funny statement. That's part of the reason why our walks always took a long time. I always knew when the climax of the story was coming because we slowed down and would stop even if we were in the middle of a street.

I wanted to take a shower and clean up before going down to talk to Sr. Jane. I managed a fast shower, then sat in the living room with Sr. Annie and Sr. Jane as she told us stories of her brothers during World War II back when they were all children.

"There was a German prisoner camp near our house," Sr. Jane said. "Often kids around the neighborhood came to watch the prisoners play soccer because we had never seen such a sport. We didn't mean any harm; it was just fun to watch them play games on weekends. Anyway, my two brothers Drew and Guy and three other neighborhood boys took a couple of Roman candles and one night drove a car to the edge of the German prisoners' camp. Drew and Guy were just thirteen or fourteen years old, and they were always mischievous. They were just kids, and they were less mature than the teenagers we have now. They shot the Roman candles, which lit up the sky above the camp. The Germans, who were about to go to bed, thought the fireworks signaled their freedom. They all got up and ran to escape.

"The American soldiers and militia in charge of the camp had to turn on all the lights and use large speakerphones to tell the prisoners to stay calm and stand still or they could be shot. The loudspeakers said that the fireworks did not signal anything. Frightened, the boys rushed back to their car and drove as fast as they could back home to escape the commotion they had caused. They were so white-faced with fear that when they sneaked back into the house, they rushed to their rooms, put on their pajamas and pretended to sleep. The sheriff of the town soon came knocking on our door, and I answered the door.

'Is your father around?' Sheriff Robinson asked.

'Yessir,' I said, and I called my father.

'I need to speak to your two sons.'

So my father called Drew and Guy to come down. They put on a show all right with their yawns and rubbing of their eyes, pretending they had just been asleep.

'Where have you two been tonight?' The sheriff asked.

'We were sleeping sir,' Guy said.

'Are you sure? Did you not go somewhere?'

'No sir.' The younger one, Drew, started to be agitated.

'If you hear anything unusual, let me know,' the sheriff told our father.

"The next morning at breakfast Father asked Drew and Guy again where they had been last night. 'I told you, we were sleeping,' Guy said, but seeing that his little brother was about to break down through sheer nervousness, he told father the truth about the night before. Immediately, Father took them to the sheriff's office and told them to 'tell Sheriff Robinson exactly what you just told me.'

"After this episode, the German prisoner's camp was off limits to us, even on weekends, so there was no more watching soccer games. It became a funny episode later because people could have been killed due to Drew and Guy's innocent prank."

Sr. Jane went on a couple more minutes about other times when Drew and Guy got into trouble. One was a story about their throwing snowballs at passing cars. They even pelted a police car, so their father had to get the boys from the police that day. Sr. Jane told many stories, as did Sr. Annie.

Sr. Francesca called me so I got to hear her voice again before leaving Taiwan. She thanked me for coming to Taiwan, and she specifically told me to thank my parents who were "generous enough to share their daughter with us." She said many of the nurses and old people asked where I went, and they all miss me. I was so glad to hear it. I thanked her for taking me to Tainan and planning it so I stayed there the longest. Tainan was the best community for me.

3/11

I had set my alarm to go off at 4:50 in the morning because departure time had to be 5:30 in order to make it to the airport on time. At least, I thought I set it at the right time. Sr. Susanna knocked on my door in the morning saying, "Caroline are you coming to the airport with us?"

I felt odd since I was the one who should have been thanking them instead of the other way around.

I was confused, as my alarm hadn't gone off, but when I checked the time it was 5:15. My mind went blank, but immediately I knew what the cause was. I forgot to set it for 4:50 a.m., and the default for the alarm is p.m.. I didn't even have time to be mad at myself as I ran to the bathroom and rushed to do all the last minute packing and saying of goodbyes. But I somehow did it all within those fifteen minutes.

The sisters I said goodbye to, except for Sr. Annie, were the ones I have seen and known only the past few days in Taipei. I didn't help them much with their work, but they thanked me for coming to Taiwan and giving them "new perspectives and fresh attitudes." I felt odd since I was the one who should have been thanking them instead of the other way around. Sr. Annie's goodbye was kind, short, and joyful. She told me to write her, to keep in touch through mail. I promised I would, hugged her, and said I much appreciated and enjoyed her company, and I loved all her stories.

We got to the airport with plenty of time. Sr. Susanna and Sr. Magdalene were the ones who were to send me off, and we ate breakfast at one of the cafés in the airport. I bought them breakfast.

I had plenty of reflection time at the airport with Sister Susanna. I have written down many of my experiences in Taiwan, but perhaps the best stories are ones unwritten because words feel too uncertain, too vague to capture how I felt about them.

At every goodbye in all the communities I have visited, the sisters and the nurses have thanked me before I could even begin to express my own gratitude. While we had breakfast, Sr. Susanna told a story that helped me understand why so many people were determined to thank me.

When Sr. Susanna was young and busy, she helped administer a hospital where there were many old people. She kept busy running from the home to the pediatric center, doing all sorts of chores to keep the hospital running. At the time there was an elderly sister who had no administrative job, a woman who has since died.

She went to each patient's room where she complained that her leg hurt, so she sat in patients' rooms for a while and visited with each one. She did this daily. The person the patients remembered best was the old sister who came every day with her hurting leg. Patients did not remember the administrator who kept the lights on at night until a specific time or the nurses who helped them stay clean and checked their vital signs, who made sure they were physically well. The one most helpful, everyone said, was the person who took the time to talk to and get to know the patients on a personal level. Checking blood, and making sure everyone gets food and medicine—these are important. But without the elderly sister who complained about her leg, the one who established personal relationships with the old people, the patients felt that what others did to help them physically was essentially pointless. Those who provided only physical care were merely working in another business.

Sr. Susanna said that through my stay at each home for the elderly I have, without intending to, so reminded each sister of the importance of relationship in tending to the aged.

Sr. Susanna said that through my stay at each home for the

elderly I have, without intending to, so reminded each sister of the importance of relationship in tending to the aged. So I became that sister with the hurt leg, one who helped refocus upon relationships in the daily routines and busy schedules.

I thanked the Sisters of Charity for how they took care of me, for I felt truly appreciated and could tell they would miss me. I came to help, but if Sr. Susanna was right, then I may have helped those who didn't think they needed any help in the first place.

I forget sometimes I am eighteen. It is a surprise to me to know my young energy and freshness was a help. I felt useless sometimes because I didn't know what chores I should be doing. But I don't feel useless anymore. Sr. Susanna said that the sisters who helped the poor everyday, the nurses and all those involved in the caregiving need to be reminded that their work is precious, to be reminded never to take the humanity, charity, and justice out of their work. She said I served as such a reminder.

"Travel in other cultures stretches you," my friend said, "and the new you might not fit well in your old surroundings." But I felt no such thing.

Suddenly, it was time for me to go. Everything went smoothly, and my plane ride felt so short that before I knew it I landed in the Osaka airport. As I walked down the crowded airport hallways and looked about me and heard the familiar gossipy Japanese and breathed in the familiar fresh air, I couldn't help smiling. And when I saw my family, when I walked through the doors of my home, I felt such fulfillment and satisfaction. I had been afraid my Chinese experiences would change something in me, that "home" in Japan somehow wouldn't feel like it once did. A friend once said once you travel outside your home, returning will be difficult, that you will notice much you never saw before and things that used to matter may not matter anymore. "Travel in other cultures stretches you," my friend said, "and the new you might not fit well in your old surroundings." But I felt no such thing. I have never felt so much joy and appreciation for my home than I do today. The emptiness I feared was instead fulfillment. I knew I was home.

03/15

It has been four days since I returned from Taiwan, and now is the time for me to finish my Chinese journal. I have fit into my family as easily as I ever had. My life has not turned upside down as I feared, and I am back to being the older sister, the daughter, and the friend on weekends. There is little doubt that I have changed. Perhaps it will be those around me who must adjust to me, as my change is something spiritual, something not so palpable. My personality has not changed, my face has not changed, but the aura I feel within has become different, and I hope I have become wiser if only in a few ways. Speaking of Taiwan now makes me feel like I am dream-ing or recounting a dream, and all those days of hardship seem not hard at all. In some ways my life in Taiwan seems like a beautiful dream. But it was not; it was real, and my experiences there will surely always be bookmarked in the many chapters of my life.

Before I end this journal I must thank my parents for making my dream to go to Taiwan possible, and I feel such gratitude to Daughters of Charity in Japan for helping me make connections with the sisters in Taiwan. I must thank all the sisters and all the people who have taught me so many lessons, ones I will apply to my daily life. Finally and ultimately I thank God, for through Him everything is possible.

www.ingramcontent.com/pod-product-compliance
Lightning Source LLC
Chambersburg PA
CBHW022021090426
42739CB00006BA/230

* 9 7 8 0 9 8 2 7 5 1 4 9 7 *